# CELEBRATING
## the
## CALGARY EXHIBITION
## & STAMPEDE

### The Story of the Greatest Outdoor Show on Earth

# CELEBRATING
## the
## CALGARY EXHIBITION & STAMPEDE

# The Story of the Greatest Outdoor Show on Earth

## Joan Dixon and Tracey Read
## ALTITUDE PUBLISHING

**This book was written to honour Alberta's Provincial Centennial and is dedicated to all the volunteers and staff members who keep Guy Weadick's dream of the Stampede alive.**

### Acknowledgments

Steve Allan, Karen Brimacombe, Winston Bruce, Robin Burwash, Dale Butterwick, Warren Connell, Maureen Cremer, Anita Crowshoe, Dr. Reg Crowshoe, Hugh Dempsey, Hilary Dolhaine, Gord Fache, Max Foran, Lindsey Galloway, Ron Getty, Raymond Goodman, Charlie Gray, Mary Halpen, Kristen Higgins, Linda Jacobson, Vern Kimball, Catherine Laycraft, Keith Marrington, Teri McKinnon, Helen Miles, Jayne Nicholson, Sherry Patram, Val Robinson, Brian Rusted, Laurie Schild, Don Stewart, Hal Wetherup, Mike Whittle, Joan Wilson

**Published by Altitude Publishing Canada Ltd.**
1500 Railway Ave., Canmore, Alberta  T1W 1P6
www.altitudepublishing.com
1-800-957-6888

| | |
|---|---|
| Art Direction: | Stephen Hutchings |
| Design and layout: | Scott Manktelow and Stephen Hutchings |
| Index: | Elizabeth Bell |

We acknowledge the financial support of the Government of Canada through the Book Publishing Industry Development Program (BPIDP) for our publishing activities.

**Altitude GreenTree Program**
Altitude will plant two trees for every tree used in the manufacturing of this book.

### Library and Archives Canada Cataloguing in Publication

Dixon, Joan, 1957- ; Read, Tracey, 1946
      Celebrating the Calgary Exhibition & Stampede : the story
of the greatest outdoor show on earth / Joan Dixon and Tracey Read

Includes  index.
ISBN 1-55153-939-X

1. Calgary Stampede--History.  2. Calgary (Alta.)--History.
I. Title.

GV1834.56.C22C3 2006      791.8′4′09712338      C2005-906730-6

Printed and bound in Canada by Friesen Printers      2 4 6 8 9 7 5 3 1

**Front cover:**
This photograph from the early days of the Stampede shows Flores LaDue demonstrating her skills as a superb horsewoman. Flores was the wife of Guy Weadick, the founder of the Calgary Stampede.

**Back cover:**
Saddle bronc riding is one of the Calgary Stampede's signature rodeo events.

# Table of Contents

The Phenomenon of the Calgary Exhibition & Stampede . 7

# The Phenomenon of the Calgary Exhibition & Stampede

In an address on the occasion of the centenary of the province of Alberta, former premier Peter Lougheed said that, in his opinion, the Calgary Exhibition & Stampede is the third most significant event in Alberta's history — surpassed only by the gaining of provincial status and the discovery of oil.

Indeed, there is nothing in the world like the Calgary Exhibition & Stampede. From its humble beginnings as an agricultural fair, it has earned its reputation as "the Greatest Outdoor Show on Earth" through more than 100 years of celebrating the west — the old west, the wild west and, more recently, the new west.

Complex and eccentric, the organization known far and wide simply as "the Stampede" has served as a reflection and expression of Calgary's changing times and culture, adapting to challenges while staying true to its mandate to preserve and promote western heritage and values. The brilliant vision to blend the original agricultural exhibition with a frontier celebration resulted in a unique and amazingly long-lasting festival that has touched people in the 19th, 20th, and 21st centuries.

The Stampede festival attracts well over 1 million visitors annually; more than half of these are from Calgary and the surrounding area. Local guests look forward to each year's celebration. They know what to expect from their old friend — the heart-stopping action of the Rodeo, the awesome power of the chuckwagon races, a spectacular Evening Grandstand Show, world-class agriculture activities, the adrenalin-pumping midway rides, and a variety of programs.

First-time visitors from other places are amazed when they compare the spectacle to their fairs or festivals back home. While the midway and displays might be familiar, the scope, size, and spirit of the Calgary Stampede outstrip any other annual fair experience imaginable.

People who have experienced Stampede from the inside — everyone from committee volunteers, rodeo competitors, staff members, Young Canadians performers, and grandstand ushers — see the 10 days and the Calgary Exhibition & Stampede in different ways than the public. They suggest that when you're involved even just a little, you take it to heart. The spirit of Stampede is in these people and in the story of the west.

The history of the Stampede and its growth demonstrate that it is an organization holding true to its roots. The key elements were there from the earliest days — the parade, the Rodeo, the chuckwagon races, the Indian Village, displays, agriculture events, spectacular entertainment, and the participation of the entire city in the celebration — and flourish to this day.

What has emerged from the fair's long history is a spirited not-for-profit organization whose goal is to be at the heart and soul of the west — not just during 10 days in July, but all year round — by fostering western pride, civic identity, and volunteerism. This vision to be the community's gathering place is bearing fruit: more than 2 million people visit Stampede Park throughout the year to participate in hundreds of events.

Given the Stampede's long tradition, steeped in western heritage and values, supporters and fans worldwide can expect it to maintain its iconic status far into the 21st century.

*– Steve Allan*
*Chairman of the Board and President,*
*Calgary Exhibition & Stampede*
*2005*

# chapter one

# The Stampede Experience

## Parade rituals

Getting up with the roosters, pulling on cowboy boots, and dusting off hats retrieved from the back of the closet — for thousands of people, these rituals spell the start of the annual pilgrimage to downtown Calgary to experience the parade that kicks off the annual 10-day Stampede. Every year, weather is one of the biggest question marks for parade day. Fortunately, Calgarians are accustomed to dressing for any weather, even if parkas and blankets must join the boots and hats as part of their outfits.

Snagging a prime curb location — preferably the same spot every year — is one of the goals of a successful parade expedition. This determination to secure a clear view of the parade is a tradition. In the early days, parade goers sat on wooden boxes bought for 10¢ from the Chinese-owned grocery stores on 7th Avenue. Some sat on the roofs of buildings overlooking the route or even climbed telephone poles for bird's-eye views.

Every year, people get downtown earlier and earlier. Some will even camp out the night before if they are the designated placeholders for a large group, or they'll lock lawn chairs to lampposts to reserve their families' spots. Staking out one's territory is a tradition not easily forsaken, in spite of the recent availability of reserved bleacher seats.

The first parades in Calgary were associated with the exhibitions held in the early 1900s and were historical pageants on a grand scale. Then as now, the parade was synonymous with the Exhibition and Stampede experience — many would even say their enjoyment of the festival today would be incomplete without it.

The modern parade is a two-hour celebration of the Stampede and its place in the city. Its unique western theme permeates the city. About 400,000 spectators line the route, and a Canadian television audience of 2 million is joined by countless millions more viewers around the globe, courtesy of numerous international media outlets. Of all the world's parades, the Rose Bowl is the only one larger than the Stampede's. On parade morning, most downtown offices and businesses are closed, and people spill onto the streets to celebrate the beginning of another Calgary Stampede.

## What they've been waiting for

The Stampede parade has always provided tremendous free entertainment. In its modern iteration, the pre-parade entertainment — including dancers of all kinds and nationalities, the Stampede's Band of Outriders, martial arts experts, and magicians — warms up the crowd.

To help the police maintain the safety of the crowd and the parade participants, deputized volunteer marshals are stationed along the route. Competing informally to work on the best-behaved block, many volunteers ask for the same assignment year after year, having developed a rapport with the "regulars." As he choreographs his section's "yahoos," volunteer Basil Nobbs, a 73-year-old former Royal Marine, learns to count "1, 2, 3" in Russian, Taiwanese, and Chinese. Such multicultural community building is another ritual, another Stampede tradition.

At precisely 8:55 a.m., the warmed-up and now wide-awake crowd hears the familiar sound of a marching band. The award-winning Calgary Stampede Showband has led the parade since 1971, its members attired in red and white uniforms.

In the distance is the tell-tale clip-clop of the first horses. In the early days, there were thousands of horses in the much-anticipated parades. This focus on the horse has continued, with about 850 "parade-broke" horses in the spectacle in an average year. And right behind each entry is the necessary clean-up crew.

Coming up next? Many more bands and dozens of floats, with entries varying from year to year. Cowboys and space-men. Miniature donkeys and chuckwag-ons. Tiny Shriner airplanes. Politicians and clowns. Water guns and princesses. Pipe bands and dancing music. Members of the Treaty 7 First Nations dressed in traditional regalia, their horses with beaded adornments as beautiful as their riders'.

A glittering display … and the partici-pants know it. The proud paraders brim with characteristic western friendliness and find it surprisingly easy to connect with celebrants sharing their spirit on these city streets.

The parade is the annual ceremonial kickoff to a community celebration that takes back the west for 10 days every July.

## The first Stampede parade

By 1912, Calgary had a track record of producing inspiring parades for its Exhi-bitions. Calgary's population may have been only about 60,000 at the time, but more than 75,000 enthusiastic spectators lined the streets on a warm and sunny September 2 to watch the "Grandest Pag-eant of All History" — the parade that kicked off Guy Weadick's first Stampede. A welcome arch was erected on Centre Street between 8th and 9th Avenues to greet the governor general and his wife. The parade was filmed and shown all over the world, setting the standard for legendary Stampede parades.

Weadick's parade portrayed the history of the west in a chronological tableau format featuring sections of missionaries

**Opposite:** Calgary Stampede Showband

**Above:** Showband brass

**Above:** The Governor General of Canada, HRH the Duke of Connaught, and his wife, pass through the triumphal arch that was temporarily installed on 8th Avenue for the first Stampede in 1912.

**Below:** The Victory Stampede parade in 1919 drew thousands of spectators into the streets.

**Above:** Natives from the Treaty 7 First Nations were an important part of the Stampede from its earliest days.

**Below:** A group of cowboys and cowgirls poses on the street to watch the Stampede.

From year to year the parade marshal reflects the interests of the community.
In 1965, Walt Disney had the honour of leading the parade.

**The parade marshal** at the head of the 4.5-kilometre-long parade is important for what he or she symbolizes. In the early days, there wasn't a choice for parade marshal: it was always Cappy Smart. As the fire chief in a frontier town, Cappy was a very important person and one of the Exhibition's organizers. He always made sure the parade was on time, and he led his last one — on foot as usual — only two weeks before he died, in 1939.

After Cappy, there was no logical regular successor, so it became the Stampede president's prerogative to pick the honorary parade marshal. The marshal can be a member of royalty, a politician, sports hero, Hollywood celebrity, astronaut, businessperson, or native chief. He or she can lead by car or carriage or on horseback. The only times there haven't been a marshal were during the two world wars, out of respect for the times and for the forces serving abroad.

Every year, the president keeps his choice under wraps until the kick-off party for the media, three weeks before the Stampede. Longtime Stampede volunteer Diane Anderson recalls that the most exciting part of her childhood Stampedes was finding out who was going to lead the parade. Would she recognize him or her from TV?

The year actor Duncan Renaldo from the popular 1950s western show "The Cisco Kid" gave her an autographed picture tops all her Stampede memories.

Other noteworthy parade marshals include:
- Albertan Daryl Sutter, general manager and coach of the Calgary Flames, and Ken King, president and CEO, shared the honour to celebrate their hockey team going to the Stanley Cup finals in 2004
- Walt Disney and Mickey and Minnie Mouse
- Politicians such as Premiers Peter Lougheed and Ralph Klein and Prime Minister Pierre Trudeau
- Heroes such as pilot Punch Dickins, astronaut Chris Hadfield, and Canadian sports figures Nancy Greene and Ken Read
- Guy Weadick, on the Stampede's 40th anniversary
- Native chiefs and Prince Charles, to celebrate the 100th anniversary of the signing of Treaty 7
- Cowboys, of course, such as Herman Linder, who first competed in 1928, and Iris Glass, the matriarch of the chuckwagon racing family; and TV cowboys, such as Jack Palance

and Hudson's Bay traders in Red River carts, old-time whisky traders, North-West Mounted Police veterans from 1874 (labelled the "old mounties"), cowboys and cattlemen, stagecoaches and settlers, with the young "citizens of the future" bringing up the rear.

Leading the way, almost 2,000 native people in full ceremonial dress created one of the parade's most impressive entries. They had come to participate in the parade and the Rodeo, to camp and visit and celebrate.

The governor general of Canada and his family stayed with the Lougheed family and were invited to ride in their host's car. In the lead section was Johnny Mitchell, the first mayor to wear a five-gallon Stetson and start Calgarians' tradition of dressing western. He was no cowboy, but he knew his city and how deeply rooted the area's western heritage was.

## Parade traditions

The Stampede parade has seen some interesting traditions come and go, while some have endured.

- Through 1950, the "first white woman in the west" was always an honoured participant.
- Contests for the best-dressed cowgirl and cowboy saw Flores LaDue (Mrs. Guy Weadick) win in 1912 and the Herron ranching/oil family in 1946, when they wore the first *white* felt hats made by Smithbilt, introducing the symbol of the west that resonates to this day.
- Cowboys on horses liked to lasso unsuspecting spectators for fun.
- Runaway horses provided some of the biggest excitement. Until riders were ordered to keep them in the centre of the street, horses wandered and were easily spooked by crowds.
- During the 1940s, cattle herding was part of the parade, but the potential for a stampede resulted in that short-lived

**Above:** A clown prepares for the upcoming events.

tradition being abandoned.

- Chuckwagons have been in the lineup since 1923. Troy Dorchester, the talented wagon driver who followed in his father's footsteps, remembers standing between his dad's knees holding the lines as they drove the parade route.

### The Parade committee

The Stampede parade is the result of the efforts of hundreds of volunteers who devote thousands of hours to the signature event to bring it to fruition. Hundreds of potential entries are evaluated and selections made, hours of meetings determine the myriad details that must be communicated. At last the entries are placed in their final order and the parade is ready to go. A barbecue for volunteers and participants the night before the parade is the committee's way of saying thank you to everyone who has worked so hard to bring it all together.

On parade day, the committee chairman weaves through the parade in his golf cart, politely but firmly making sure all is going well with participants and spectators and ensuring that no parade crashers ruin the fun for everyone else. The chairman and his marshals also keep their eye out for skittish horses or young children, who might dash unexpectedly onto the parade route.

Less than an hour after the parade is completed, the volunteer committee meets over lunch for a quick evaluation. The 100-plus member group, which includes generations of the same families, reviews the morning and proposes ideas to make the parade better next year.

### "Stampeding"

At the end of the two-hour extravaganza, parade goers are ready for doing, rather than watching. The entire family and city can participate in the western celebration. It's what makes the Calgary Stampede unique in the world. Free breakfasts

**Above:** A Scottish pipe band in full regalia

**Opposite top:** 2005 Stampede Queen, Lauren MacLennan leads her two princesses, Coleen Crowe and Justine Milner.

**Opposite bottom:** The antics of numerous parade volunteers keep the audience excited.

**Above:** Part of the enthusiastic parade audience

**Opposite:** A last minute photograph before boarding a float for the parade

are served at community halls or off the backs of chuckwagons downtown, with Roy Rogers lookalikes, politicians, and CEOs flipping pancakes. There's line or square dancing in Rope Square downtown and street parties all over town.

If people use a little imagination, the city might even resemble an old western town. Straw bales, rough lumber, and wagon wheels create false storefronts, and enthusiastic urban cowboys dress in boots and jeans as if they were competing in the bull riding that afternoon.

Indeed, nobody in Calgary has to look too far to find the key components of western wear — cowboy boots and hats, jeans, belts with decorative silver buckles. Dressing western is a great equalizer, as it was during the old days on the range, blurring the distinctions between ranch bosses and ranch hands. Real cowboy duds may be more faded or worn than those worn only during Stampede, but tens of thousands of urban Calgarians get into the spirit by dressing west-

ern. "If you're in Calgary during those 10 days — you'll know Stampede's here!" says Phil Heerema, who works with the Grandstand Show.

## On to the Park

Stepping through the gates of the Greatest Outdoor Show on Earth, visitors are welcomed by volunteer ambassadors or hospitable Howdies to a place that offers an evocative western atmosphere. At one end of the Park is Weadickville, a reconstruction of a frontier town, and at the other end, an Indian teepee encampment with 100 years of history.

First impressions of the Stampede can be overwhelming. There's so much to see and do! Some people prepare by reading the Daily Events Schedule in advance and planning their itineraries accordingly. Some folks prefer to be spontaneous, while others visit their favourite attractions in the same order every year. No matter what the plan, it's

## Weather dependent

**Snow, rain, wind, hail, or extreme heat** — it isn't a typical Stampede without at least one fierce afternoon thunderstorm during the week. Just like Alberta farmers, who say they live and die by the weather, organizers of the 10-day festival wonder all year what July will bring — two days of rain can make a huge difference at the gate and to the bottom line.

Most Calgarians can recount their own worst weather day or year at Stampede. Here are some of the more notable historical incidents:

- Massive rainstorms postponed the Exhibition as early as 1890, making roads impassable. Again in 1925, heavy rains created havoc.
- In 1929, a flash flood drowned the Park.
- Near-freezing temperatures were reported for at least two nights in 1934.
- Hailstones greeted Prime Minister St. Laurent in 1950, also the year of a disastrous flood of the Park.
- A blizzard accompanied the command performance for Princess Elizabeth and Prince Philip in October 1951.

inevitable they'll stumble onto something different, as there are always new attractions.

The Stampede prides itself on offering something for everyone. In the great outdoor Samaritan Suntree Park, musical and other acts have been entertaining for several decades. More recently, Nashville North started attracting long lineups of country music fans.

For young children, there is Buckaroos, a play area in the Big Four Building, as well as their own ride area on the midway. On Kids Day, the youngsters and their parents get into the Park free and enjoy a free breakfast, modified rodeo, and special entertainment. There's one ride both children and parents can do together: the Skyride gives a bird's-eye view of the whole Park and moves people from one end of the midway to the other — a happy solution for tired feet.

From the earliest days, the midway has drawn people to the Park, helping to underwrite the fair financially as

well as attracting the younger crowd. A 1908 photo of the midway shows a variety of booths that would be at home at the modern festival — palm reading and ice cream cones were as popular then as now. Among the shouts of barkers and the smell of popcorn, kids go on thrilling rides, visit horror houses, and shoot at tin ducks, the lucky ones taking home prizes that draw envious stares from less successful contestants.

Rarely does anyone go away hungry. Fair food offers everything from cotton candy, mini doughnuts, and corn dogs to cappuccinos, paninis, and smoothies. The many booths now compete for best of the midway awards. And to keep it all clean, an army of Boys & Girls Club members stays busy sweeping up the crumbs while earning valuable work experience.

The Stampede Showband and its smaller breakout groups play all over the Park; one photo-friendly location is the steps of the Pengrowth Saddledome.

Their vast repertoire and the beat of the drumming from the Indian Village compete with the incessant question, "Have you bought your ticket yet?" Calling out "If you don't play, you can't win" from lottery booths all over the Park, members of service clubs raise hundreds of thousands of dollars for charity and give away life-changing prizes.

Permanent buildings and temporary tents house many diverse components. The Corral and Pengrowth Saddledome are the sites of such Stampede favourites as Western Performance Horse shows, mini chuckwagon races, and stock dog trials. The Roundup Centre features the latest household gadgets expertly pitched by travelling salespeople, just as in the fair's old days. Here also can be found Western Showcase — featuring the arts, crafts, and entertainment of both the old and new wests. The unique Western Art Auction attracts hundreds of serious art collectors and raises funds for the Calgary Stampede Foundation.

**Above:** The Stampede midway at night

**Opposite:** The cowboy hat is the icon of the Canadian cowboy.

Stampede offers urbanites a rare opportunity to introduce their children to the wonders of the animal world in the agriculture displays. Under the Big Top and in the livestock barn, the smell of hay and manure is ever-present, with huge bulls and hundreds of horses being groomed for their shows, as they have been at every fair since 1886. Newer to the Stampede are the llamas, miniature horses, and donkeys that enthral young and old alike.

Living up to its billing as the Greatest Outdoor Show on Earth, the Stampede features its signature events – the Rodeo, chuckwagon races, and Evening Grandstand Show — outside at the huge grandstand. Here, events can be enjoyed from air-conditioned comfort inside or on sun-drenched seating outside. Fireworks have ended Stampede evenings since 1905 — and were spectacularly doubled for the province's 2005 centennial celebrations.

By midnight, unfamiliar cowboy boots are likely letting the feet know it's time to hit the hay — especially with another nine days of stampeding left! And morning will come early, with the prospect of free pancakes and sausages at one of many Stampede breakfasts around town.

Stampede-time memories like these are woven into the fabric of Calgarians' lives: their first time going to the midway, when it was covered with sawdust instead of concrete; meeting their future spouses at the huge clock tower that once stood at the centre of the Park; and bringing their own kids to the grounds. In spite of the incredible growth of the 10-day fair, Calgarians agree that Stampede organizers have kept the magic of the past.

**Above and Opposite:**
For many visitors, the midway is a central part of the Stampede experience. From midway food that includes corndogs, caramel apples and candyfloss to the spills and thrills of a multitude of midway rides, there is never an empty stomach or a dull moment.

# chapter two

# Historical Highlights

## The Beginning

For almost 100 years, Calgary has been celebrating its existence at the edge of the western frontier by roping off its streets, setting up straw bales, and inviting its citizens to dress as cowboys and cowgirls. Even — or possibly especially — its urban folk get a kick out of the annual conversion to a turn-of-the-20th-century cowtown. Since 1912, this metropolis has developed its know-how for putting on the most ambitious of western celebrations.

For millennia, the confluence of the Bow and Elbow Rivers was familiar to the Nations of the Blackfoot Confederacy, which hunted the buffalo that gathered in the sheltering coulees by the crystal-clear waters. Later, the fur traders came, then missionaries, whisky traders, and enterprising farmers. Shortly thereafter, in 1875, the North-West Mounted Police, charged with bringing law and order to the frontier, built a fort at Calgary. The west was waiting for the next chapter in its history to unfold.

## It all started with a bucking horse

With the arrival of the railway and the revised Dominion Lands Act in 1883 came greater opportunity for settlement and farming. On August 6, 1884, when Calgary was but a raw town, an editorial in the *Calgary Daily Herald* proposed that an agricultural exhibition be organized to showcase the area's crop-growing potential. The few farmers already established in the region were reporting astonishing crops and anticipating even better.

That year, a fortuitous accident led to the purchase of land that would become the fairgrounds. A. M. Burgess, Canada's minister of agriculture, was inspecting experimental farms in the Fish Creek area when he was bucked off his horse and broke his collarbone. He was invited to recuperate at the home of the Calgary citizen who rescued him, Colonel James Walker.

Colonel Walker was a ranch manager but also president of the newly formed Calgary and District Agricultural Society. He was determined to arrange land for a fall fair similar to the ones new Calgarians had enjoyed in their former communities. Walker convinced his guest to facilitate the purchase of 94 acres of Crown land for $235. The land, bounded on two sides by the Elbow River, made an ideal location for the fair — far from the centre of town at that time.

## The travelling exhibitions

Even though only about 100 homesteading families lived in the two-year-old tent and shack town, early Calgarians were keen to share and promote their successes and potential. As a result, the Calgary and District Agricultural Society formed a partnership with Canadian Pacific Railway (CPR) in 1884 to prepare a display that would fire the imaginations of potential settlers in the east.

The plan worked. The fine grain crops and king-sized vegetables of Sam Livingston, the area's first farmer, and Colonel Walker's tall oat crop astonished easterners, who suspected the wily westerners of splicing two stalks of wheat together to create the impressive six-foot-tall sheaves. The travelling agriculture display was so successful that it was sent east again the next year, because security concerns during the Northwest Rebellion prevented townspeople from holding their own fair at home.

**Opposite:** Guy Weadick, the cowboy visionary and dreamer whose persistence made the Calgary Stampede a reality

**Above:** This early view of the Stampede grounds shows the Industrial Building (constructed for the 1908 Dominion Exhibition), the Grandstand and the racetrack.

## The growth of the fair

By 1886, Calgary's population had risen to 2,000 people, the town was attracting investment and attention, and support for a fall fair in the area was renewed. Since the new grounds were not yet developed, the exhibits were housed in a rented skating rink, with the livestock judging taking place in an adjacent field.

Volunteers from area businesses, farms, and ranches organized every aspect and arranged prizes totalling $900 for classes that included agricultural produce, horses, cattle, home crafts, and babies. (All three babies entered earned prizes because the judges didn't want to choose among them with their proud mothers standing by.) The fledgling fair sold out in spite of a blizzard and limited entries. Calgarians, it seemed, were destined to be passionate fair goers.

However, that momentum was quickly stalled, and for several years, Calgary was fair-less. After the 1886 fair, a fire destroyed half the growing town's business section, then a livestock-killing winter and a searingly hot summer occupied all the farmers' and ranchers' time and resources, making it difficult to establish the fair.

But true to its pioneer spirit, Calgary rebuilt in optimism and sandstone. The agricultural society moved proudly onto its own grounds in 1889. In 1891, horse racing became an integral part of the Exhibition, and in 1893, George Lane, one of the future investors in the Stampede, organized the first ranch-type competition with steer roping.

After that, a few more years of challenges — including bad weather, a weak economy, disputes between ranchers and farmers, and a crop failure — put the future of the fall fair in doubt. The mortgage secured for improvements on the grounds was foreclosed, and the society ceased to operate. The grounds reverted to cow pasture and served as a field for the occasional sporting contest. Area

"THE STAMPEDE" CALGARY, ALTA 1912. OFFICIAL PHOTO N° 41.
MARCELL

WATCHING THE PARADE

farmers organized their own unofficial events during the fair-less years of 1896 to 1898, and some Calgarians worried that the "modern" new century was to be the end of the Calgary fair and its focus on agriculture — this despite that fact that livestock was still regularly driven through the streets of the newly incorporated city.

However, in 1898 the tide turned: a bumper crop was harvested and the CPR made Calgary a divisional point for the continental railway, resulting in another boom time for the city. The truly modern urban comforts of electricity, water, and sewer systems were now available to urban dwellers.

## The first Exhibition

In 1899, the Calgary and District Agricultural Society was revived as the Inter-Western Pacific Exhibition Company. The future prime minister of Canada, R. B. Bennett, had acquired the neglected fairgrounds as speculative property when the society foreclosed, but a restriction on the land title meant the grounds couldn't be subdivided or sold as town lots. He eventually sold the prime land to the city, which named it Victoria Park, after the beloved deceased queen. The city renewed the lease, and improvements were made to the fairgrounds and buildings.

Midsummer replaced the traditional fall time for the renewal of the celebration. Another key change featured industrial and commercial development side by side with agriculture, to reflect Calgary's diversifying economy. Trick roping, wild horse races, and midway attractions were added for their entertainment value and ability to drive revenue.

The city rallied behind the newly invigorated fair, and every year seemed to bring new innovations. In 1900, 2500 of Calgary's 4,000 residents attended to bet on the horse races and try out the new sideshow amusement park. In 1903, a full-time Exhibition manager

**Above:** The 1912 Stampede parade drew thousands of Calgarians and visitors in to the streets. The old City Hall is in the background.

## The Big Four – George Lane

**Part of the Stampede's** organizing committee from the beginning, George Lane was a pioneer cattleman who had followed the cattle herds up from the United States. By 1892, after working as the foreman at the famous Bar U Ranch in the Longview area, Lane had put sufficient money aside to purchase his own ranch, the Y. T., south of High River. In 1893, he expanded his holdings by purchasing the Flying E Ranch.

Lane supplied meat to Pat Burns' meat-packing operation, and by 1900 was in the position to buy the Bar U with a number of partners. The ranch became famous for the quality of its Percheron horses. While owner of the Bar U Ranch, Lane introduced branding chutes and corrals to facilitate ranching operations. As one of the Big Four, he considered the Stampede the perfect way to show off the achievements and potential of the growing, progressive west as well as celebrate its frontier past. In 1913, Lane became the member of the provincial legislature for the riding of Bow Valley. When he died in 1925, the *Calgary Daily Herald* called him "the most colourful character in Alberta's Ranching history."

was appointed as ranching and farming activities in the area became solidly established and the fair continued to grow. Fireworks were featured to celebrate Alberta becoming a province in 1905 and became a tradition.

Putting the brakes on the boom, the worst winter on record — "the Big Stink" of 1906/07, with its staggering losses of livestock — ended the era of open-range ranching. The future suddenly looked grim for Calgary's ranchers and cowboys.

## The great Dominion Exhibition

In 1908, with a population of 25,000, Calgary was awarded the Dominion Exhibition, a federally funded fair that moved from metropolis to metropolis each year. The city was determined to showcase its regional production. A budget of $145,000 in government grants created an explosion of construction: six new pavilions and a properly built racetrack with a roofed wooden grandstand were quickly designed and built.

Over a period of seven days, and despite terrible weather and a severe economic depression, more than 100,000 people entered the fairgrounds. Thousands of Americans came from as far away as Spokane on special trains to celebrate their Fourth of July in the heart of the new west. The Miller brothers' 101 Ranch Real Wild West Show traveled north from Montana in a 45-car train, and — as fate would have it — one of the cowboys aboard was trick roper Guy Weadick. The troupe performed three shows under its own canvas tent one day and left the next, but Weadick's interest in the area's potential had been sparked.

One of the other unique new attractions to awe 1908 Exhibition visitors was a hydrogen-filled, propeller-driven balloon called Strobel's airship. It made five successful flights over Victoria Park. On the sixth attempt, a gust of wind caught the airship and drove it against the grandstand, where it exploded and burned, fortunately without casualties.

A historical pageant that was 6.5 kilometres long defied expectation, with floats of every ethnic group, hundreds of native people, countless marching bands, and dignitaries that included Lieutenant Governor George Bulyea and Senator James Lougheed. A total of 2500 animals were entered in the judged competitions, and more than 40 communities and the four western provinces had displays. In addition to the exhibition classics, there were also an art exhibit, an all-female band, acrobats, a wild animal circus, a polo game, and vaudeville entertainment.

The decidedly western theme honoured the ranching life: the exhibits were in an area called the Corral, the midway was called the Roundup, and Western Day featured cowboy contests and Indian races. The format of agricultural and industrial exhibits alongside major attractions such as a wild west show and the midway seemed to work very well.

Although Calgary's potential as "the" wild west show location was immediately obvious to Guy Weadick, for the next few years the annual event remained primarily a static display of agricultural products, animals, and machinery. The city was losing its western spirit, even prohibiting traditional impromptu bucking contests on its downtown streets.

By 1911, aviation and autos had become the fair's new attractions, and horse racing adopted pari-mutuel betting as Calgary began evolving from a market town to a commercial and industrial centre. Once again the city was booming. Its population grew to 63,000 and streetcars appeared. The Inter-Western Pacific Exhibition Company's name had changed to the Calgary Industrial Exhibition Company, suggesting a significant change to the horse-centred fair.

## The first Stampede

Not everyone was convinced Calgary had to turn its back on its agricultural and rural heritage in order to grow. Guy Weadick returned to the city in 1912 and boldly proposed a new event, a spectacular Stampede to celebrate the romance of the quickly vanishing original west. His idea was to differentiate his show from other frontier days, rodeos, and roundups.

## Weadick's story

Once in a long while, a person comes along with a crystal-clear vision that becomes a fundamental part of a community's sense of identity. Guy Weadick was such a person. An easy-going, affable man, Weadick had a gift for forging life-long friendships. He lived a charmed life during the great transition from the era of open-range ranching to the smaller scale of agriculture that replaced it. The romance of this time fueled his visionary's fervour to capture the moment before it vanished.

Born in 1885 and raised in Rochester, New York, Weadick was fascinated by the west as it was presented in the travelling wild west shows. As a teenager, he went west to Montana and by the age of 20 was an experienced working cowboy, well versed in the cowboy arts. In 1904, while in Alberta to buy horses, he was an enthralled visitor at a Sun Dance ceremony in Standoff and later in the year attended a rodeo in Cardston. He never forgot the images these events impressed upon him, nor the contacts and friends he made.

His experience as a working cowboy made it possible for Weadick to enter the world of wild west shows — theatrical tent shows that featured re-enactments of Indian battles and stagecoach robberies as well as demonstrations of ranching skills such as trick roping. Weadick partnered with the legendary steer wrestler Bill Pickett, and in 1905, they attended the Calgary Exhibition. By then, he was one-quarter cowboy and three-quarters showman.

Weadick had a passion to celebrate the romance of the old west but in a more authentic fashion than that of the wild west shows. His vision entailed less focus on vaudeville entertainment and more on pure rodeo events, and he was convinced southern Alberta was fertile ground for the spectacle he had in mind. In 1908, he came to town to perform in the Dominion Exhibition and discussed his dream with several key businessmen, but the time wasn't right.

By that time, Weadick had married Flores LaDue, a beautiful and spirited trick rider and fancy roper. For the next few years, they were featured on the wild west show circuit, travelling as far afield as Paris, where, on a famous bet, Weadick took his horse up three elevators to the top of the Eiffel Tower.

However, something in the spirit of Calgary sat in Weadick's mind and drew him back in 1912. He convinced the Exhibition's general manager, Ernie Richardson, and stock supplier Addison Day that his dream of a great Stampede was worth considering. Financial backing was the key. The idea was a go when four prominent Calgary businessmen and ranchers — Pat Burns, A. E. Cross, George Lane, and Archie McLean — agreed to support the venture if necessary. All they asked of Weadick was to "make it the greatest thing of its kind in the world; we don't want to lose money, but we would rather lose and have it right, than make money and fail in our objectives."

## Weadick did it right.

With his first successful Stampede under his belt, Weadick's passion for the old west grew. His talents as a performer and organizer were in great demand, from Winnipeg to New York. In 1919, Richardson invited Weadick back to Calgary to stage a Victory Stampede celebrating the end of World War I.

In 1920, Weadick and LaDue bought a working ranch west of High River with the dream of making it into a dude ranch. They called it the Stampede Ranch (not to be mistaken for the ranch the Stampede owns today), and over the years, it became a mecca for cowboys and celebrities alike. While the Weadicks' itinerant lifestyle as travelling performers continued, the Stampede Ranch was the home to which they returned each year after the show circuit ended.

Then, in 1923, as the Exhibition was facing a decline in popularity, Weadick was asked to merge the Stampede with the Exhibition — and history tells the rest of the story. As the manager of the Stampede, Weadick continued to honour the area's ranching roots and its pioneer spirit. One of his legacies is the annual Rangemen's Dinner, which he started in 1929 with the assistance of Canadian Pacific Railway.

Sometimes Weadick's strong personality and passion for his vision clashed with people's understanding of the organization's needs, but he managed the Stampede until 1932, when the Depression reduced his dream and spending powers. Weadick and the Calgary Exhibition & Stampede parted ways, and he worked for other organizations on a contract basis and ran his ranch with LaDue.

After LaDue passed away in 1951, Weadick married Dolly Mullens Mott, a family friend. Weadick and Dolly were invited to the Stampede on the occasion of its 40th anniversary, in 1952. He was 67 years old and still characteristically witty and charming. Recognized as the Stampede's true visionary, Weadick rode in the parade and handed out awards. He was pleased to see that prizes had doubled since his day and that the chuckwagon races, his addition to the 1923 Stampede, had become the biggest draw next to saddle bronc riding.

Weadick's second marriage was not a success — he missed his longtime partner — and the couple separated in 1953. Several months later, Weadick passed away. At his funeral, his favourite horse, Snip (a gift from the Big Four), walked riderless, Weadick's boots backward in the stirrups. The dreamer is buried in the High River cemetery, where his grave marker reads "Guy George Weadick, founder of the Calgary Stampede and loyal son of his adopted west."

The force of Guy Weadick's personality and his nostalgia for the romance of the era of the open range had shaped his vision into an enduring form — and perhaps the greatest rodeo of them all. Personally, he exemplified the western values of handshake honesty, neighbourliness, and entrepreneurship that continue to define the western community. He was successful because he understood that as much as things change, sometimes the way things don't change is important, too.

To honour the man who started it all, the Calgary Exhibition & Stampede named its frontier village Weadickville and created the Guy Weadick Award. This coveted trophy is given to the rodeo or chuckwagon cowboy or cowgirl who Stampede volunteers think best represents outstanding accomplishment in his or her sport, as well as demonstrating traits such as a warm personality and sports-manship.

### Flores LaDue — Mrs. Weadick

Flores LaDue (or Florence, born Grace Maud Bensell in 1883 in Montevideo, Minnesota) was a daring woman for her time. As a young woman, she left the comfort of her family home for an uncertain future in the world of entertainment, where she used her skill as a rider as her calling card. She met Guy Weadick in Chicago when they were performing individually in a wild west show. Weadick followed her to Iowa and, after a whirlwind five-week courtship, they married.

A superb horsewoman and a natural beauty, LaDue specialized in fancy and trick roping. She and Weadick created an act that featured roping, horses, and Weadick's charming banter. Their stage names varied from "Weadick and LaDue" to the "Stampede Riders" to "Wild West Stunts," and they built a satisfying measure of fame on the entertainment circuit. In 1908, working for the Miller brothers' 101 Ranch Real Wild West Show, they came to Calgary for the Dominion Exhibition. At the first great Stampede in 1912, she won the title of World Champion Lady Fancy Roper.

LaDue was the perfect partner for Weadick, and theirs was a shared dream. They worked together in all their endeavours, and the pattern of her life mirrored his. With her practical nature, she was instrumental in their ranch's success.

**Flores LaDue – 1912 World Champion Lady Fancy Roper**

In 1946, LaDue was hospitalized briefly, and after her release, the Weadicks made the difficult decision to sell the Stampede Ranch and move into High River. In 1950, they decided to retire to Phoenix and were given a moving and heartfelt farewell — and a gift of $10,000 — by more than 300 people who wished to express their high regard.

LaDue and Weadick's ties to High River brought them back the next year for a visit, during which LaDue died unexpectedly. She is buried in the cemetery in High River. Weadick's simple tribute to her on her grave marker says it all: "A true partner."

**Above:** Automobile racing was briefly introduced during the war years of World War I.

**Opposite:** In 1919, Fred McCall was forced to crash his biplane onto the top of the merry-go-round when the engine stalled. His two passengers, the sons of the Exhibition's general manager, were unharmed in the incident.

At least four of Calgary's leading businessmen, who had made their money in cattle, were still enthusiastic about round-ups and the cowboy life. George Lane, A. E. Cross, Pat Burns, and Archie McLean — now famously known as the Big Four — listened to Weadick's proposal and backed him to the tune of $25,000 each should he need to call upon them in the event the Stampede was not financially successful. The group planned to use the Exhibition grounds in September 1912, following the summer agricultural fair.

Guy Weadick was a rodeo performer on his way to becoming a promotional genius. He dedicated the celebration to "the dying race — the cowboy," although his native friends were to play a big part, too. According to Weadick, the Stampede would re-create the "atmosphere of the frontier days of the west as they really were, devoid of circus tinsel and far fetched fiction, in an annual re-union of truly western pioneers, which would also include competitions of the daring sports of the real cowboys of the western range." His supporters were intrigued, telling him, "Spare no expense, make it the best in the world and a square deal for all." Soon, Calgary's trademark became "Whoopee!" as Weadick planned the Rodeo. Even though professional rodeo was new in Canada, Calgarians built a rodeo arena. Weadick brought out the wildest stock of bucking horses available. With prizes of $20,000 in gold, 150 competitors flocked from Manitoba, Saskatchewan, and Alberta.

Weadick also encouraged American cowboys to join in the fun. "The money is here, come and get it," he wrote to his compatriots. Three days before opening day, arena director Addison Day imported two railway cars full of American and Mexican cowboys directly from the Cheyenne Frontier Days. This may have cost $6,000, but the best talent was assembled, ready to solve the great argument — which country produced the best cowboys?

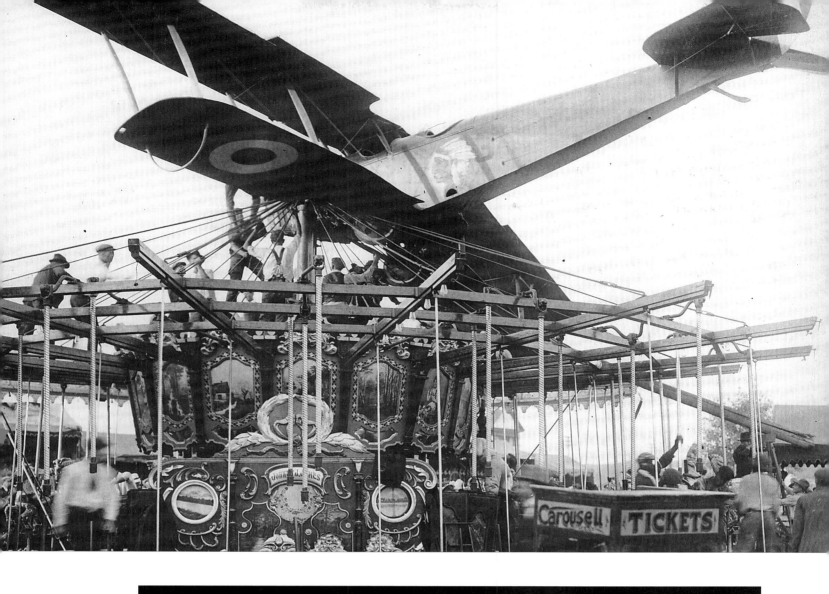

## The Big Four – Patrick Burns

**Patrick Burns** was born in Oshawa, Upper Canada, the son of Irish immigrants. The family moved to Manitoba in 1878, where as a young man Burns became a cattle dealer. By 1890, he was based in Calgary, where he established a meat-packing firm called P. Burns and Co. Ltd. Eventually this business became one of the most successful in the west, expanding to include branches in London, Liverpool, and Yokohama.

A highly regarded member of the community, Burns held directorships in several important banking, engineering, and insurance companies. In 1931, the popular Calgarian's birthday and appointment to the Senate were celebrated during Stampede. Senator Burns died in Calgary in 1937.

"CALGARY STAMPEDE"

## The Big Four – Archie (A. J.) McLean

**A cowpuncher from Ontario,** Archie McLean became a successful rancher in the Taber area. Initially disinterested in politics, he was convinced to run in the 1909 election in his home riding and won, determined to make a substantial contribution to public life. As a member of the provincial Liberal government, he served from 1909 to 1921 in a variety of positions, including provincial secretary, minister of municipal affairs, and minister of public works. In the last position, he was instrumental in the creation of the provincial highway system.

McLean became one of the Big Four unwittingly. In 1912, knowing the depth of McLean's commitment to his community and to ranching, George Lane, Pat Burns, and A. E. Cross included him in their project to pledge support for the first Stampede without consulting him.

This first Stampede premiered with a parade that featured thousands of horses, with tens of thousands of people lining the streets. The Stampede itself was a cowboy's dream — a wild west show without the glitz and sham of wild west shows. However, some of the authenticity was not as popular with spectators. Herds of cattle roamed the streets. Without chutes or time limits, rodeo events were not always spectator-friendly — it could take 10 minutes before a cowboy got bucked off, and by then, the action might have wandered far from the grandstand. And it all came at a cost. The admission fee was $1 — the highest ever — and 25,000 people, less than half the city's population, attended the special event.

Despite this low attendance, some organizational detractions, and poor weather, the Stampede experiment was deemed a success. But only Weadick and the stock suppliers made any money, so there was no repeat performance in Calgary the next year. Weadick tried to export the Stampede to other centres, but a 1913 version in Winnipeg didn't take, nor did an attempt in New York. The Stampede could not be reproduced.

## The Exhibition takes root

The 1913 Calgary Industrial Exhibition was more successful than ever. It attracted a record attendance of 104,529 (5,000 more than the previous year), 1251 exhibitors, and $100,000 in receipts. Thanks to the Turner Valley oil strike and resulting boom, an ambitious 50-year plan of expansion was unveiled. At the time, the eight-storey Palliser Hotel, the tallest building west of Toronto, was rising only a few blocks from the circle of teepees and cowboys riding horses.

When another economic depression, then World War I began, the Exhibition tried to ensure business as usual, but it was naturally influenced by political and economic circumstances outside its gates. Four thousand troops (many of them cowboys) marched in the 1915 parade. With war came technological and industrial developments, which were naturally

featured at the fair. When auto races were introduced, people wondered about the direction of the former agricultural fair.

Despite concerns, Victoria Park had developed into the year-round headquarters for many livestock associations' annual shows and sales. General manager Ernie Richardson was still determined to hold on to the Exhibition's original mandate and backbone — agriculture. But he was also prepared to embrace the new.

## The Victory Stampede

Guy Weadick was also determined to turn the fair into something even more ambitious — a permanent frontier days festival. In 1919, he was invited to plan a Victory Stampede as "a reunion of old timers in the great west," once again to follow the annual Exhibition. He advertised it in his rodeo column in vaudeville's *Billboard* magazine.

Along with the familiar, the Victory Stampede brought in all kinds of new entertainment, including the aeroplane. Pilot Fred McCall landed his unexpectedly on the merry-go-round. Wop May performed loop-the-loops over the grounds. The rodeo events continued to be popular, especially when Calgarian Clem Gardner was crowned the all-round champion cowboy. Edward, the Prince of Wales, was so delighted with his visit, he bought a ranch in the foothills so he could continue to play cowboy.

With Weadick having the benefit of more experience this time around and Victoria Park having a concrete, fireproof grandstand able to seat 5,000, the second Stampede attracted 53,456 spectators.

## A merger to celebrate

In an effort to attract and entertain Calgarians, the Exhibition developed additional creative projects — but sometimes the elements had other plans. A 1921 attempt to create a winter carnival, complete with a ski jump constructed on the grandstand roof, was foiled thanks to the weather. After a chinook melted all the snow, truckloads of snow were hauled in from the mountains and packed up onto

**Opposite:** The First Nations have played an important role from the very earliest days of the Stampede. A row of teepees provides the backdrop in this photograph from the Indian Village.

**Above:** Strobel's airship makes a scheduled landing. It made five successful flights during the 1908 Stampede before a gust of wind drove it against the grandstand where it exploded and burned — fortunately with no loss of life.

the jump. But just as the event was starting, a blizzard blew in. The entire project failed and the resulting loss had to be written off over 10 years.

By the 1920s, attendance at the Exhibition was declining. In 1922, E. L. Richardson, the Exhibition's general manager, approached Weadick and proposed that the Stampede be developed and merged with the fair. The showman, immediately grasping the idea's potential, negotiated a six-month contract, which sowed the seeds for his life's passion.

A new corporate entity, the Calgary Exhibition & Stampede and Buffalo Barbecue, presented a six-day-long combination of the Exhibition and Stampede in the summer of 1923 that focused on agriculture and ranching. Even the entertainment was drawn mainly from the truly western sport of rodeo instead of from imported vaudeville acts.

The event's 5-kilometre-long parade featured no less than five bands and 2,000 participants. They were all led by

Mayor George Webster, who, despite his urban background, happily duded up and set the tone for Cowtown, allowing Calgary's downtown to be closed off for two hours every morning for street dancing.

This was the year that Guy Weadick's inspiration resulted in western dress, store decoration, and native people becoming integral elements of the Stampede's western spirit. The first Stampede breakfast was introduced. Alongside the new chuckwagon races were wild horse races and wild cow milking. Steer roping from cars made for novel entertainment.

Cowboys proved to be great entertainment on and off the grounds, as well. They practised rope tricks downtown on office stenographers. One day, cowboy contestant Eddie King rode his horse into a café.

Spectators numbered 138,950, and the organization made a real profit for a change: $22,000. With a skeleton staff, the fair had employed as many rodeo cowboys as possible, so the gamble

STEER SAYS GOOD-BYE    CALGARY STAMPED

## The Big Four – A. E. (Alfred Ernest) Cross

**The son of a prominent Montreal judge,** A. E. Cross arrived in Calgary in 1884 after graduating from the Ontario Agricultural College. He settled on the A7 Ranch near Nanton, which became the largest ranch in Alberta. Cross became a prominent businessman with an impressive résumé — he was Calgary's first bona fide millionaire, owner of the Calgary Brewing Company, founder of Calgary Petroleum Products, a member of such premier organizations as the Ranchmen's Club, and one of the Big Four. His interest in public service led him to be a founding member of the Alberta Exhibition Association.

**Above:** This photograph attests to the fact that bull riding, one of the most difficult of the modern day rodeo events, has never been easy or without frequent sudden conclusions.

paid off in other ways, too. In the spirit of range hospitality, where no one ever went away hungry, 10,000 were served barbecued buffalo at the closing event. Buffalo robes were given to the oldest man and the oldest woman born in western Canada and a buffalo head to the longest resident of western Canada in attendance.

The outstanding follow-up success in 1924 ensured that the merger became permanent: 167,000 attended the six-day show. The Stampede perfectly complemented Calgary's Exhibition. Obviously, there was more to it than cowboys and bucking horses, but celebrating western heritage through the Rodeo proved to be a theme inextricably linked to the history of Calgary in times of boom and bust. Calgary enjoyed the old spirit of confidence and community spirit the event rekindled.

## Ups and downs

Along with the Stampede, the Turner Valley oil boom helped to counteract some of the effects of the Depression years in Alberta. As well, newfangled cars made it easier for more people to travel to the Stampede even though Calgary's streets remained unpaved and muddy for some years. In 1935, Prime Minister (and former owner of the grounds) R. B. Bennett came home to Calgary to open the Stampede.

Regardless, the attendance and receipts of the Calgary Exhibition & Stampede were disappointing for most of the hard-luck decade of worldwide depression. Fire in 1931 had again caused damage and necessitated costly rebuilding on the fairgrounds. Vaudeville was no longer the attraction it had been, fighting strong competition from the "talkies." Worse, against Weadick's advice, the newly renamed Calgary Exhibition & Stampede Company economized on attractions and prizes, reflecting the financial unease of the times. Fortunately, agriculture activities remained stable, with the organization continuing to serve the cattle, horse, and other animal markets.

By 1942, servicemen were featured participants. Unlike Toronto's Canadian National Exhibition, which closed during the war, the Stampede offered everyone an escape. Its popularity soon outstripped its facilities. A special Visitor's Bureau was established, and the new industry of tourism started to make the Stampede prosperous again. Attendance figures were 300,000 — almost three times Calgary's population.

Riding the spirit, radio personality then mayor Don Mackay led a Stampeder Special railcar to cheer on the 1948 Calgary Stampeders football team in Toronto for the Grey Cup, accompanied by six horses and a chuckwagon. Toronto was so amused by the famous Stampede breakfasts and other demonstrations of western spirit that 250 Torontonians came to Calgary the next year to experience the event in person.

In 1949, 65 percent of Calgary's population attended Stampede, many in the new Calgary fashion of white (not the traditional cream) cowboy hats, which had become the mayor's welcoming gift for dignitaries. They witnessed other symbolic changes in the festival's entertainment, such as a cowboy roping his calf from a Royal Canadian Air Force helicopter. The organization was becoming ambitious, with budgets for revenues and expenditures in the range of half a million dollars.

## Growing pains in the 1950s

In the book *Calgary, 1875–1950: A Souvenir of Calgary's 75th Anniversary*, the Stampede of the 1950s was described as "nostalgia in technicolor" and categorized with two other outstanding international outdoor events of the day — the World Series and the Indianapolis 500. This country fair was firmly in the big leagues.

With this success came growing pains. The facilities were constantly in need of repair or expansion. There were never enough horse barns. The Big Four Building and the Corral were only in the planning stages, years away from easing the crunch. As well, weather — in the form of hailstones, flooding, and a blizzard — continued to affect the

**Above:** Chuckwagons race onto the track during an early Stampede.

**Below:** Native bareback horse racing was a favourite event in the first years of the Stampede.

**Above:** Bucking horses have always been hard to ride — an enduring challenge for rodeo contestants.

**Below:** Tilly Baldwin rides a bucking horse in 1912. Guy Weadick watches the action from horseback.

**Above:** The Industrial Building was constructed in 1908 for the Dominion Exhibition. It was destroyed in May, 1931, by a fire of unknown origin.

Greatest Outdoor Show on Earth in the early 1950s.

It was good news and bad news in 1952. Foot and mouth disease struck farmers in the never-ending cycle of hardships in the agricultural industry. However, Calgary's streets were finally being paved, and Guy Weadick returned as an honoured guest to celebrate the Stampede's continued success.

However, overall, the 1950s were good to the city and the Stampede. TV and the ease of modern travel stimulated interest in the west and encouraged tourism. Calgary had become an oil capital, with plenty of American immigrants catching the Stampede spirit. As the festival expanded further into the world of entertainment, there were fireworks every night. Hollywood stars such as Bob Hope and Bing Crosby headlined shows and led parades. Rodeo was in its heyday, with the colourful bronc riding star Casey Tibbs at the peak of his fame.

## Popular themes of the 1960s

By 1960, things were certainly changing from the days of Guy Weadick. The ticket price included a free outdoor show. Although gambling was still not permitted, charitable raffles became popular and the tradition of the Dream House lottery began. The Big Four Building, completed in 1959, was air-conditioned thanks to its curling rinks. The brand-new Stampede Ranch was raising its first foal crops, including Cindy Rocket, a mare born in 1961 and destined for rodeo greatness.

In 1962, 500,000 attendees celebrated the 50th anniversary of the first Stampede, Roy Rogers and Dale Evans among them. A $50,000 gold ingot was raffled. President H. Gordon Love commissioned and wore a frontier suit made from 10-carat gold cloth. The Grandstand Show became a regular feature during the 1960s, and 1964 was the last time wranglers brought in the rodeo horses on a bona fide trail ride. Although the Stam-

pede was busting its britches, its plan to take over Lincoln Park on the city's western boundary was not approved. That left nowhere to expand but north into Victoria Park.

The Stampede formally recognized oil's impact on the province with three-acre Flare Square and a fully operational oil rig. Oilmen and cowboys were seen to have lots in common: they were generally rugged, adventurous individuals who were willing to leave the comforts of home to break new trails.

Annual themes became popular to focus programming Park-wide. In 1966, the Stampede broke all records of attendance (654,000) and brought in a fresh crop of volunteers. Canada's Centennial in 1967 saw a popular Calgary day complete with a rodeo at Expo 67 in Montreal and the Great Centennial Balloon Race in Calgary. The same year, the festival was expanded to 9 days and the parade was moved from the Monday to the preceding Friday to open the festivities.

The next year, the Stampede expanded to 10 days, after years of struggling to accommodate all its programs and the increasing numbers of visitors. Liquor was finally allowed in the dining room. A casino moved into the Big Four. Both significant changes helped boost attendance and the Stampede's bottom line. A variety of expansion plans were seriously pursued. New livestock facilities appeared in 1968. The food services department blossomed.

## More boom and bust — the 1970s and 1980s

Rodeo Royal, the first of what would be an annual indoor spring rodeo, was introduced in March 1972 and proved popular with rodeo fans. In 1973, the Royal Canadian Mounted Police celebrated its 100th anniversary. The same year, Queen Elizabeth II visited for her second time, accompanied by Prime Minister Pierre Elliott Trudeau. In 1974, the Stampede

**Above:** This aerial photograph shows the extent to which the layout of Stampede Park has changed over the years.

expanded and the Indian Village moved to its current location at the south end of Stampede Park, along the Elbow River. A new emblem, Stampede Slim, was introduced. A grandstand designed for many uses was built at great expense.

As rodeo grew more popular, it competed for time with horse racing, and thoroughbred races had to be left out of the Stampede program after 1976. Roundup '78 proved unsuccessful as a spring livestock show and was eventually moved to October.

By the late 1970s, the oil/financial capital boom was superseding the agricultural industry. Even the Stampede's board of directors was increasing its business and professional membership as farm and ranch representation decreased. It looked like cowboy culture again risked being swallowed by urbanization. Consultants were asked to help re-establish Stampede Park as a showcase of agricultural leadership of western Canada.

By 1979, congestion had become one of the Park's biggest problems and recurrent challenges. Individual chuckwagon drivers had been soliciting corporate sponsorships for their outfits for years, and that year an official program was initiated to bring businesses into the fun of chuckwagon racing by auctioning off coveted advertising space on the tarps.

More and better facilities were still required, so a king-sized exhibits building, the Roundup Centre, was planned, along with Weadickville and Suntree Park. Land was also purchased in Victoria Park. New events were introduced. Midnight Madness attracted youths in droves.

That year, negotiations between the Stampede and the Canadian Professional Rodeo Association became deadlocked. The Stampede entered into a three-year agreement that included all the regional cowboy associations across Canada and the United States, which resulted in the 1979 and 1980 Stampede Rodeos featuring teams of cowboys, rather than individual competitors.

The 1980s saw much to celebrate. Premier Peter Lougheed and the largest powwow ever assembled in Alberta celebrated the province's 75th birthday and its proud heritage in Alberta Square in 1980. There was a Park parade every evening. In 1981, the Flames hockey team moved from Atlanta to play in the Corral while the Saddledome was under construction in preparation for the 1988 Olympics. Also in 1981, the format for the Rodeo combined team and open events. The following year, the format of all open events was re-established, which is how the Rodeo continues to operate.

In 1986, the Exhibition's centennial year, the livestock industry "hogged" the spotlight with its new hit of pig racing. Bad weather in 1987 didn't keep one million people from visiting or the new headquarters of the organization from opening. The year 1988 was the year of the Olympics. Stampede Park had buildings and a volunteer committee structure already in place to help host the massive event. The Park not only hosted hockey and figure skating events, it provided the venue for the media centre. The Stampede's Grandstand Show producer, Bill Avery, produced the medal ceremonies in Olympic Plaza with help from the Young Canadians. Hometown favourite Robin Burwash won the first Olympic Cultural Rodeo, to the great pleasure of his country and the Stampede. Inspired, the Calgary Flames won the Stanley Cup later that spring and the Stampede set an attendance record in the summer.

Aggie Days, a new attraction in 1989, was an instant hit, introducing urban school children to agriculture in an entertaining, educational way. Corporate sponsorships of the organization's activities reached a record $2 million. Discussions about the future of the Stampede initiated a planning document, Horizon 2,000. The major North American attraction was growing richer in programs and visitors, but it was bursting at the seams.

## Moving ahead — the 1990s

In 1990, the Stampede celebrated 100 years of horse racing. In an innovative new program, it capitalized on the popularity of rodeo by offering indoor rodeos year-round for corporate conferences held at Stampede Park.

The Stampede could have benefited from the Rodeo being held indoors in 1991 — it rained so much that fresh dirt had to be brought into the infield. Rain and the continuing recession attempted to dampen spirits again the next year, except at Nashville North, the new country and western venue, and at the racetrack, where simulcasting bolstered income.

In 1994 the Stampede sold its management contract for the Saddledome to the Flames for $20 million. In 1995, the Calgary Stampede Foundation was established to support youth projects. Historical murals began to adorn huge blank walls around the Park and at the airport, artistically capturing the festival's glorious past. The state-of-the-art infield facility was finished in 1997, and a sophisticated pyrotechnical laser show jazzed up the evening show. The Canadian Country Music Hall of Fame found a permanent place at the Park the next year, as did the new venture of Calgary Stampede TV. Another century was just

around the corner, and the Stampede was prepared to be part of it.

## The millennium threshold

The new millennium welcomed a new attendance record of 1,218,851, with 2,000 finally breaking 1988's attendance record — one of the sure signs of continued growth. The Roundup Centre was expanded just in time for the many millennium events. The building's huge trade show hall, large banquet facility, breakout rooms, and elegant public areas continue to make the Stampede a popular destination for corporate and private functions. The Bull Sale celebrated its centennial in 2001. The Stampede hosted the world championships of both the Six Horse Hitch and Marching Showbands.

In 2004, a Master Plan was launched to manage growth in Victoria Park in the 21st century. The organization plans to consolidate its role as a gathering place for the community.

**Above:** An early Grandstand crowd awaits the start of the rodeo events.

# chapter three

# Indian Village and the Treaty 7 First Nations

## The ancient western culture

Nomads without borders, the natives living on the great plains had followed the buffalo for food and essentials of life from time immemorial. When horses descended from stock introduced to the continent by Spanish conquistadors became naturalized across the west, natives developed one of the great horse cultures of the world. By the mid-1700s, horsemanship had become a preeminent component of Plains Indian culture — horses were a measure of wealth, and an important contributor to the communities' livelihood.

The Royal Proclamation of 1763 recognized the native tribes as rightful occupiers of their hunting grounds, endearing the Crown forever to them. In 1867, the British North America Act gave the federal government responsibility for the region's native residents and created Queen Victoria as their royal protector.

For millennia, countless herds of buffalo had sustained the way of life of the Plains natives. Their nomadic culture had evolved to harmonize with the migration cycles of the buffalo, which fulfilled virtually every need for food, shelter, and clothing. With the coming of settlement, buffalo were hunted in vast numbers to satisfy the markets of the east and Europe. When the demand for buffalo hides reached its peak in the late 1800s, the herds neared extinction across both the Canadian and American plains. With this catastrophic and unforeseen development, the traditional migratory way of life of native peoples was doomed.

When traders of illegal whisky began taking advantage of the native peoples, the government sent the North-West Mounted Police to bring order to the west. It was in an atmosphere of relative law and order that native leaders signed Treaty 7 at Crowfoot Crossing, east of Calgary, in 1877, which set aside reserves, promised annual payments, and provided farming supplies to compensate for the land required for the railway.

Within a short period of time, agricultural settlement of the area around Calgary began, and social organizations based on European traditions were transplanted. Relationships between the native population and immigrant settlers were established.

## At the Calgary Exhibition

The people of the Treaty 7 First Nations have been involved with the Calgary Exhibition & Stampede since its earliest days. As the years passed, involvement in Calgary's agricultural fair and the Stampede provided the venue and the opportunity for the people to gather in a social environment that sustained age-old cultural practices.

From the start, native people came to Calgary's agricultural fairs to share in the celebration by providing dances. In return, the Stampede offered gifts of food items such as tea and flour. In 1903, Cappy Smart organized a special Indian Sports Day for the Exhibition.

However, the government had concerns regarding native people gathering and expressing their culture as a group. It soon discouraged their participation, believing it would be better for native people to give up their nomadic and traditional culture, stay on their reserves, and learn

to farm. Reverend John McDougall, the Methodist missionary to the Stoney Indians, disagreed, regarding any cross-cultural opportunities to be educational. He supported and supervised native participation in the Dominion Exhibition pageant in 1908 and in 1910, when the fair staged a re-enactment of the signing of Treaty 7, with thousands of native people taking part in the five-act play.

## At the Calgary Stampede

For the first Stampede in 1912, Guy Weadick's vision was to portray the history of the old west by featuring both cowboys and native people. Because the government was reluctant to issue permission for the natives to leave their reservations for extended periods of time, Weadick turned to Calgarians Sir James Lougheed and R. B. Bennett, who used their influence with the federal government to ensure that native people could participate. Weadick's visionary commitment

to the native community set a standard for inclusiveness that helped the Treaty 7 First Nations sustain their culture.

Under the supervision of Reverend McDougall once again, almost 2,000 native people left their reserves to participate in the Stampede. They competed in Indian races, offered daily dances as part of the celebrations of the old west, and displayed their finest traditional dress, tools, and horse regalia in the ambitious parade. A classic and spectacular war dance was performed in the arena for the Grandstand Show.

Ben Calf Robe, an old friend of Weadick's, recalled 20 families of his Siksika Nation being granted permission to move their ceremonial teepees to Calgary's fairgrounds. As one of the few of his people who could speak English, 23-year-old Calf Robe became the first (and longest-serving) interpreter at the Calgary Stampede, explaining the white man's festival to the Siksika while sharing some of his people's traditions

**Above:** A line of teepees in a native encampment during the early 1900s

**Opposite:** Young native Canadians in full costume perform a traditional dance.

with fair goers. Calf Robe wrote of his appreciation for the side of the grandstand reserved for native people free of charge, so the two cultures could share their love of horse racing.

From 1919 to 1922, there was still no native participation permitted in the Exhibitions. Weadick had to again pull strings to arrange permission for native participation in 1923 — the Stampede was about to merge with the Exhibition and audiences expected to see the popular native people.

In 1925, the outright ban on fair participation was modified to allow Elders to attend the combined Exhibition & Stampede on the occasion of the 50th anniversary of the arrival of the North-West Mounted Police. By 1933, a new government administrator, M. Christensen, finally cancelled all restrictions and authorized full participation. He joined the Stampede's board of directors, established special exhibitions of native handicrafts, and encouraged teepees to be open for public viewing.

Primarily providing a place for the people to live during the early fairs, the Indian Village evolved into a place that

## The Indian Events Committee

**The Indian Events committee** meets throughout the year to work out plans for the annual Stampede Indian Village. To honour the blending of cultures, Elders begin and close the meetings with prayers in their native languages.

Before 1970, there were no native people on the committee, but many (including teepee owners) are now actively involved, ensuring more equal opportunities to share in everything the Village provides. It is by common agreement and to recognize the historical relationship between the Stampede and the Treaty 7 First Nations that the term "Indian" continues to be used.

Bruce Starlight, a Tsuu T'ina teepee owner, feels that native involvement is a vital part of Stampede history. Starlight ran successfully for the board of directors in 1992 and served until 1997. During his tenure, Starlight lobbied behind the scenes for the increased involvement of native people and particularly native youth, to ensure that native culture remains vital and that the Village is supported in the future.

honours native heritage and educates the public by offering rare glimpses into native life and culture prior to the arrival of the first settlers. Without the Village encouraging the preservation of these important customs, many people believe their traditions might have been lost. Raised on the Tsuu T'ina reserve, Bruce Starlight is one of the believers. "That's why natives participate in it — because we're very concerned about preserving our ways. If it wasn't for the Stampede, we wouldn't have the things we still do as a people today."

When the original Indian Village became too crowded during the 1930s, teepee owners were asked to help choose the family teepees that best represented their tribes. These became the keystones for future Village participation. From then until 1950, the Village had 30 teepees — 10 each from the Siksika, Stoney, and Tsuu T'ina Nations.

Originally, all native people holding Treaty cards were welcomed at the Stampede free of charge, even if they weren't teepee owners or their guests. Eventually, complaints about the open-door policy led the Stampede to provide free entry and food only to registered Village participants.

Misunderstanding the purpose of the change, the unhappy Stoneys boycotted the Stampede in 1950. Coincidentally, that year produced torrential rainstorms that flooded the Village and its events. The media had a field day, speculating whether the Stoneys' rain dances were responsible for the weather. Eventually the Stoneys returned to the Stampede, and in the early 1960s, the Blood (Kainai) and Peigan (Piikani) Nations became official participants as well.

The Stampede began offering honoraria in addition to provisions to help offset expenses incurred in setting up and hosting the Indian Village. In 1971, the Indian Buffalo Ride was introduced at the Rodeo to showcase the native people's historical attachment to the icon of the

**Above:** A crowd fills the entrance to the Indian Village.

**Opposite:** In this historic photo, teepees and a teepee frame stand outside a Hudson's Bay building.

**Above:** A native hoop dancer performs at the Grandstand.

**Overleaf :** A native dancer is lost in a fantastic blur of feathers, colour and movement.

plains and to try to create an enhanced role for native people at the Rodeo.

The Indian Village was moved in 1974 from its location near the Corral to a quieter, more protected spot near the river at the south end of the Park. Historically, it remains the only summer camp in North America where different Nations share the same ground at a fair.

In 1977, Treaty 7's 100th anniversary was celebrated, with the five Nations leading the parade along with Queen Victoria's great-grandsons, Princes Charles and Andrew. A pre-Stampede parade, symbolic of traditional nomadic rides, involved 120 native people riding horses from the grounds through the downtown core. Twice as many teepees as usual were set up, along with a 12-metre-wide Council teepee. A formal interpretive program that included a look at the contemporary side of reserve life made its first appearance that year.

When the Stampede saluted native people in 1999, the Indian Events committee organized more contemporary cultural exhibitions, including an Aboriginal Film Festival. Even as the Village adapts and evolves, former member of the Indian Events committee (now Stampede life member) and historian Hugh Dempsey says, "some things never change:" everyone shares the excitement of the formal opening as they dress for the parade in their "business suits."

## Preserving and sharing the past

The Indian Village is one of the most popular Stampede attractions for visitors, mainly because it is one of the few venues where authentic native culture is accessible and celebrated by both native and non-native people who appreciate the benefits of its cross-cultural knowledge exchanges.

The Indian Village is also popular as a social gathering for the participants, providing much-anticipated reunions every summer. Over the years, Elders have been able to share their traditions with their families, the other nations, and non-natives.

Third- and fourth-generation children of the original teepee owners now play and dance together, continuing their Elders' traditions. They are extremely busy throughout Stampede, riding in the parade and Rodeo, participating in the flag raising ceremonies, demonstrating dancing or drumming, exhibiting their handicrafts, making or selling bannock, having their pictures taken by enthralled tourists, and answering curious visitors' questions.

As Herman Many Guns of the Piikani Nation says, "The more we know about each other, the better things work out." Many Guns and the Starlight family of the Tsuu T'ina Nation have come to welcome the opportunity to demonstrate their pride in their Nations' distinct customs.

During the 10 days of Stampede, teepee owners and their families erect and open their symbolically decorated teepees and encourage people to participate in events that sustain links to the past at the same time as they provide opportunities for learning and understanding. They demonstrate games, drumming, singing, dancing, meat cutting skills, crafts, and teepee raising and prepare traditional foods such as bannock, berry tea, and pemmican jerky.

Statistics show that nearly one-fifth of all people coming to Stampede visit the Indian Village, so in any year, more than 150,000 guests enjoy the hospitality of the Treaty 7 First Nations and come to understand native culture in an atmosphere of celebration. Over the last century, native participation in the Stampede has evolved from merely providing entertainment to preserving and sharing their rich cultural heritage.

## The Stampede Powwow

The annual Stampede Powwow is a dance competition attracting some of the best native dancers on the continent. Just as in the old days, the dancers and drummer-singers share their incomparable

# Teepees

The Indian Village

**One of the most visible elements** of native heritage is the teepee. During Stampede at the Indian Village, 27 teepees are set up in a circle around an imposing flag pole with the huge colourful designs of the various Nations dominating the grassy open. Because they are used as living spaces, the teepees are open for viewing on a rotating schedule.

The right to own one of the beautiful teepees is considered an honour and a tradition that families generally pass down through the generations. Since the early days, the teepees have competed to be named Best in Camp and are judged on everything from size, design, the displays inside and out, and the beadwork and buckskin work demonstrations inside. Prizes inspire high standards and also confer family and tribal pride.

The teepees' symbolic designs come from dreams. The bottom band, usually painted brown or red, symbolizes the earth. The large middle area's colour is determined by the dream's setting. The top band is usually black to symbolize the night sky from whence the dreams come. What connects the original dreams to individual people is the practice of transferring each teepee's design through a transfer ceremony to its next owner, a time-honoured ceremony conducted for generations.

For the past decade, a daily teepee raising competition has challenged teams to set up camp quickly and efficiently. The impressive speed with which teepees are dismantled, moved, and re-erected celebrates the ancient need to move camps to follow the buffalo herds across the prairie or to find shelter and fuel.

A large Council teepee, located in the centre of the circle, provides the venue for formal meetings between the First Nations and their invited guests. A number of ceremonial teas are held each summer to honour special guests of the Elders, such as members of the Stampede's board of directors.

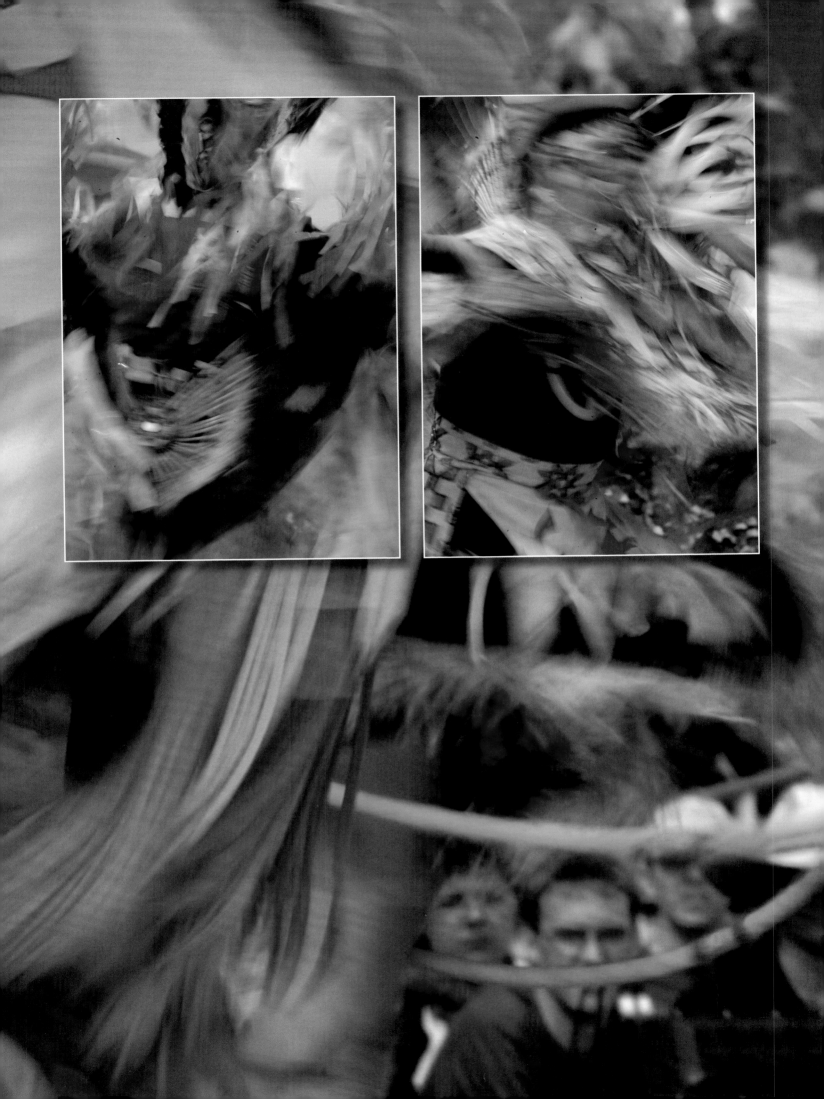

# Traditional foods from the Indian Village

## Bannock on a stick

Bannock was introduced when traders brought flour, salt, lard, and baking powder. These ingredients were mixed together and often cooked in kettles, also brought by the traders. Alternatively, the dough was wrapped around slim green branches and cooked over an open fire.

| | | |
|---|---|---|
| 6 cups | flour | 1.5 L |
| 7 tbsp. | baking powder | 105 mL |
| 1 tsp. | salt | 5 mL |
| 1/2 cup | flour (keep separate for dusting) | 125 mL |
| 4 cups | water | 1 L |
| 1 | willow stick, 3 ft (1 m) long and peeled at tip | 1 |

(Vary the amounts of flour and water according to how sticky you like the dough.)

Mix together dry ingredients. Make a hollow in the centre. Add water in the hollow and stir until the ingredients are just mixed (overmixing will make the dough hard and tough). Knead dough lightly. Sprinkle flour on sticky spots. Knead lightly again until all spots are covered with flour.

Pinch off a piece of dough about the size of a softball. Stretch it out to about 1 foot (30 cm) in length. Place the peeled part of the stick in the middle of dough lengthwise. Pinch the dough together around the stick. Holding the stick just above the flames, cook over an open fire until bannock is golden brown. Depending on the fire, this will take between 10 and 20 minutes. Make sure the dough is cooked through. Remove from the fire. Let cool slightly before eating. Bannock can be eaten either hot or cold.

## Berry soup

Berry soup played an important role in many ceremonies. Saskatoon berries were most often used in this traditional food staple.

| | | |
|---|---|---|
| 8 cups | water | 2 L |
| 6 cups | Saskatoon berries | 1.5 L |
| 1 cup | berry sugar (or regular sugar) | 250 mL |

If required for thickening:

| | | |
|---|---|---|
| 1 cup | water | 250 mL |
| 1/3 cup | flour | 75 mL |

In a large pot, bring water to a boil. Add berries and sugar and cook at medium heat for 20 minutes, stirring occasionally to make sure it doesn't stick to bottom of the pot. If the soup is too thin, mix the water and flour together so there are no lumps and gradually add to the berry mixture, stirring constantly. Additional sugar can be added to sweeten. Boil for at least another 15 to 20 minutes. Remove from heat and let stand for 5 minutes. Serve hot.

## Dry meat

A staple food source, dry meat was used as a basis for making pemmican.

| | | |
|---|---|---|
| 4 lb. | beef flank | 2 kg |
| | salt to taste | |

Wash the meat in cold water. Cut into three portions. Cut through each portion, stopping just before you separate the two pieces. The meat should open like a book. Sprinkle the pieces with salt, and hang on a wooden rack or tripod over a fire, or in the sun to dry. The drying time depends on the method of drying and weather conditions.

# Pemmican

Pemmican is well known as the quintessential Native American food. Light in weight and nutritious, it was a staple for native people, who needed a portable, reliable source of sustenance when they were on the trail or there were no animals to hunt. It could also be safely stored for relatively long periods of time, an important feature to this culture that typically could not keep its food supply cool.

As part of the interpretive program at the Stampede's Indian Village, pemmican is prepared each summer according to age-old traditions. To make pemmican, dry a quantity of meat and pound it to a powdery texture. Melt and cool animal fat, and add the rendered fat to the powdery meat until the mixture holds together. Add berries such as Saskatoons, if they are available. Wild mint can be added as an insect repellent.

**Left:** Tom Three Persons poses with his wife, Ambush Woman.
**Right:** Tom Three Persons aboard Cyclone

**The most famous rodeo cowboy** in the early 1900s was tall, rangy Tom Three Persons, a member of the Kainai (Blood) Tribe from southwestern Alberta. Naturally athletic, Three Persons learned to ride as a youth working with his stepfather, a Blood Indian rancher. As a young man, he honed his ability to ride bucking horses while working as a hired ranch hand, impressing his fellow cowboys with his talent.

A second-place finish at the 1908 Lethbridge Fair followed by a win the next year at the same fair launched Three Person's career as a bucking horse rider. In 1911, he joined Addison Day's touring wild west show and gained a measure of fame. By 1912, he was ready for the challenge of his first big international rodeo competition — the Calgary Stampede.

Three Persons rode to Calgary with a caravan from his reserve, reaching the city in three days. Although the cowboys welcomed him, he chose to camp with his people. Three Persons was the only Indian cowboy to enter the four top-rated rodeo events, a dashing figure in his fancy silk shirt, red chaps, tooled leather boots, and wide-brimmed cowboy hat.

Three Person's masterful ride on his first bronc made him eligible for the finals, for which he drew the infamous Cyclone, who'd bucked off all 129 riders who had attempted to ride him, including the world's best.

Cyclone stayed passive during his saddling but broke loose to make a circuit of the infield before being recaptured. Once Three Persons was in the saddle, the horse tried everything in his repertoire to buck him off — rearing, swapping ends, and sunfishing — but the cowboy stayed in the saddle until the judges at last told him he could dismount.

Once the ride was over, pandemonium broke out. Three Persons' supporters galloped around the arena chanting and whooping loudly, while spectators surged across the field to congratulate the rider. To everyone's amazement, the local cowboy had become the world's bucking horse champion, winning $1,000, a saddle, and a gold belt buckle. He was the only Canadian to win any of the open events.

A true trailblazer, Tom Three Persons became a hero to his people and the first of many talented professional native rodeo competitors. He was a successful calf roper for years and, through his ranching activities, became one of the wealthiest native people in Canada.

**Above:** A beautiful example of the intricate design and pattern of traditional native handicrafts.

**Opposite:** A native dancer performs at the Indian Village.

arts with non-native audiences, but now they also compete for thousands of dollars in prize money.

On the outdoor stage in the Village, daily demonstrations of drumming and dancing draw crowds enthralled by the rhythmic beat, the singing, and the gorgeous, intricately beaded regalia. The songs, body movements, and traditional dress have historical cultural meanings that an interpreter describes to the people gathered on the grassy hillside. The individual dances are related to native

societies and have their roots in different geographical areas of North America.

The Chicken dance originated on the plains — the dancers' movements mimic the dance of the prairie chicken. The intricate and colourful traditional dress symbolizes the attributes of the bird, for example the dancers' feather bustles represent the tail feathers.

The Jingle dance, which originated in the southwestern United States, is another popular feature. Women move gracefully through the movements as the announcer shares that each dress is adorned with 365 tiny tin bugles (once made from snuff-can lids), each representing a day of the year.

Throughout the powwow, light-footed and gorgeously dressed dancers range in age from tiny children just able to walk, to their Elders, who have participated in many powwows over the years. All move to the same hypnotic music of the drummer-singers.

## A unique honour

**In 2005,** the Nations of the Indian Village made Steve Allan, chairman of the board and president of the Stampede, an Honorary Chief. He was given the name Aa-koh-hkii-to-pii, which translates as "Rides Many Horses," to honour the Alberta Centennial project that saw more than 200 horses trailed overland from the Stampede Ranch at Hanna to Calgary. For two historic days, the horses and cowboys passed over the open ranges of the Siksika Nation.

# chapter four

# Ranching

## The opening of the range — boom times

While the Marquis of Lorne was touring what is now southern Alberta in 1881, he expressed the sentiments of many when he announced "If I were not Governor General of Canada, I would be a cattle rancher in Alberta." Warm chinooks and sheltering coulees, endless plains of self-perpetuating fescue grasses, and clear mountain streams enticed Europeans to the wide-open range land of Canada's west.

Cheap leases on Crown land — 100,000 acres at a penny an acre — encouraged the dreams of neophyte and experienced ranchers from many backgrounds. Within a few short years, cattlemen had taken over land that had once been the domain of free-roaming buffalo herds and their native hunters. As ranches south of the border became overcrowded with cattle and disputes over the use of the remaining range land festered, Americans, too, started looking north.

The presence of the North-West Mounted Police provided security for the cattle business, a comfort missing in the more socially independent American west. Ranchers such as George Lane mustered enormous cattle drives to bring stock, capital, and expertise to the Canadian west. Adventurous investors from England and eastern Canada contributed their purebred breeding stock. Penniless young immigrants worked alongside the wealthy sons of titled British families. Together, all these groups built the western Canadian ranching industry that the Calgary Exhibition & Stampede continues to honour.

The collaboration of all classes and races in the frontier environment underscored Alberta's fundamentally egalitarian culture. The tenants of the tent towns and ranch houses mixed socially and recreationally first in the saloons and at the horse tracks, then at regional fairs.

## The closing of the range — the bust

In a cycle that would become familiar in Calgary, just around the corner from this early cattle boom was the unforeseen bust.

When the railway reached Calgary in 1883, ranchers welcomed the new mode of transportation more for its potential to move cattle to market than they did for its ability to bring an influx of thousands of homesteaders.

At first, the homesteaders' herds wandered the open range, mixing with cattle from established ranches. Several brutally cold winters, resulting in the loss of tens of thousands of head of cattle, destroyed the myth that the west would support livestock with the same success that it had the buffalo, a species that had acclimated over millennia to withstand the prairie's harsh climate changes. Eventually the land was fenced so that individual farmers and ranchers could confine and hand feed their stock during winters, changing the dynamic of the ranching industry forever.

As wheat became the new king of exports, the cattle market softened. This, combined with shipping problems, slowed the potential of the ranching industry. In Ottawa, political support for ranching was replaced by support for farming. To ensure their survival, some ranchers turned to mixed farming.

## The cycle continues

With improved range management, the cattle industry revived. Ranching flourished in areas where farming couldn't, such as the foothills, and by 1950, beef exports again topped wheat in value. From the 1960s onward, developments in ranching, such as community livestock grazing, helped it prosper. Large tracts of land, abundant and affordable feed grains, and the natural shelter provided by southern Alberta's topography continue to support large-scale beef production. Ranching on small landholdings also contributes to the beef industry's growth and economic importance.

The boom and bust cycle continues, with BSE, a mysterious cattle disease, being the latest crisis to affect the industry. In spite of it, "ranching is as alive and well in western Canada as it was in the halcyon days of the later 19th century," suggests western historian and Stampede observer Max Foran. Half of Canada's cattle live in Alberta. Adding to the diversity of stock, exotic alpacas, llamas, and ostriches have become familiar sights on the prairie. To survive, ranchers today must be astute businesspeople with state-of-the art information and practices to manage and conserve the land.

Sustaining and supporting the west's longstanding relationship with ranching — through the good times and bad — has been a priority since the first fair. The Stampede continues to seek and maintain programs that support excellence in beef breeding with the help of such venues as the International Room in the Agriculture Building. During the 10-day festival and at other times of the year, this famous room hosts visiting dignitaries, importers, exporters, and agriculture groups for formal and informal networking.

## A hub for horses

Alberta has always been known for its horse industry. Thoroughbreds were a key part of the ranching industry at the start — these versatile horses were fast and trainable and had the stamina for the work required by the cowboys. Alberta-bred heavier breeds such as Percherons, important for their ability to haul wagons and pull the ploughs that broke the virgin prairie, were world-renowned.

But by the 1940s, working saddle horses and the teams of heavy horses had almost disappeared from the landscape. Trucks, tractors, and, later, all-terrain vehicles slowly replaced the remudas of horses. However, the horse industry has experienced a tremendous resurgence in the past few decades, and once again Alberta is famous for the quality and variety of its breeding programs.

Reflecting this significance, horse-related events are an integral part of the Stampede — at the track, in the barns and show rings, and at the Rodeo. At the Stampede Ranch, staff use horses instead of trucks for most chores, preferring to do things the old-fashioned way, just as working cowboys have done for decades.

In the Western Performance Horse events held at Stampede, the ghosts of the past are present as working horses go through their paces. Team penning has

---

### Ranching Legacies: Off to the races

**Horse racing** was always a part of the Exhibition. In 1926, in fact, instead of auto races, the more popular horse races were selected to close the show. The introduction of pari-mutuel betting in 1929 legitimized and increased racing's popularity with the masses.

But in 1976, despite the new Grandstand, leaders of the thoroughbred industry were concluding that rodeo and racing didn't mix. Thoroughbred racing was dropped from the festival but combined with harness racing and developed into a year-round sport. Live racing 100 days a year and simulcasts kept the grandstand building hopping for a while.

When video lottery terminals were introduced in the mid-1980s, the era of horse racing at Stampede Park almost ended. Young people and city folk not steeped in the nuances of horse breeding and training stopped supporting the racing industry and looked elsewhere for their entertainment. As the Stampede tried to weather the storm, its commitment to the industry and its heritage meant huge financial losses. The Alberta government now aids the sport by adding slot machine revenue into both race purses and operational expenses.

A proposal to build a new racetrack and gaming facility just north of Calgary near Balzac has been accepted by Horse Racing Alberta, and the Stampede is planning its future without this historic component of its operations.

**Above and Opposite:**
Essentially unchanged for over 100 years, attention to detail in western tack can be found in everything from the spurs on a pair of boots to the reins on a horse.

its history in feedlot and ranch work, where it was necessary to sort cattle out of herds. Working cow horses are trained to be ridden on a light rein and to move cattle where they're needed to go at a variety of speeds. In the cutting events, talented equine athletes are given minimal direction from their riders and use their natural ability to efficiently separate (cut) cattle from their herds one at a time. Their job is to overcome the instinct for cattle to return to the comfort of the group. In their competitions, reining horses display tremendous athletic ability by effortlessly changing gaits and speeds and demonstrating their stopping power.

Rodeo events also underline the importance of good horses that are well suited to their work. Powerful bucking broncs challenge cowboys in the bareback and saddle bronc events. Other horses work in tandem with their riders in tie-down roping, steer wrestling, barrel racing, and working cow horse events. Pickup men and rodeo judges also depend on their equine partners to make sure they're able to do their jobs to the best of their ability.

# chapter five

# The Stampede Ranch

## Wanted: more bucking broncs

In the heart of the short-grass ranching country near Hanna, Alberta, lies a jewel in the crown of the Stampede's many assets — the Stampede Ranch. Thousands of acres of unfenced prairie are home to the horses and bulls that make the Stampede Rodeo famous worldwide for the quality of its bucking stock.

In the early years, the stock selected to be put in the pens at Alberta's rodeos generally consisted of outlaws deemed unsuitable for saddle horse purposes. Many of their ancestors had been turned loose during the Dirty Thirties to run semi-wild across the prairie's open ranges after ranch families abandoned the land. Generations of unmanaged interbreeding produced big-boned animals with heavy horse and thoroughbred blood in their veins.

As the land was reclaimed by the next influx of ranchers, wild horses became scarce, and good bucking stock for rodeos hard to find. For a long time, the Stampede depended on ranchers and Stampede friends such as Ed Pugh to pool their wilder mounts and trail them to Calgary for the Stampede.

Eventually, the Stampede's board of directors decided it wanted to do more than ensure a reliable supply of buckers — it wanted to maintain and improve the quality of bucking horses. In 1961, the Stampede became the only major North American rodeo organization to experiment with raising its own stock. The core Ranch — 1430 acres near Hanna, 215 kilometres northeast of Calgary — was purchased for $200,000. Thousands of additional acres were leased, and the Ranch was stocked with 100 horses.

## Stampede Ranch work

The Stampede Ranch, now occupying almost 22,000 acres, is set on a rise in the middle of the vast prairie. Regrassed farmland and prime pasture land are mostly covered in natural short bunch grass native to eastern Alberta. About 450 bucking horses, 90 bulls, and 40 saddle horses live most of their pampered lives here. A full-time ranch foreman lives on site, taking care of the animals and property. Assisting him is a full-time livestock coordinator/flankman, and, during busy times, day hands from local ranches.

In line with the Calgary Exhibition & Stampede's principles, ranch hands primarily work the traditional way — on horseback. A trained dog was acquired to work with the bulls, but it's not used for the horses, for fear of spooking them.

### Ed Pugh

**Ed Pugh** was one Albertan who never missed a Stampede if he could help it. Ranching and rodeo were in his blood. Pugh's father drove chuckwagons during the Depression years, and Pugh rode broncs before going into the army. Beginning in 1946, Pugh was on the Stampede's stock crew and flagged the wooden chutes. He trailed bucking horses he'd raised into Calgary for the Stampede from 1947 until 1964, when he started helping out at the Stampede Ranch.

In 1967, Pugh became a wagon driver and, later, a respected chuckwagon racing judge. He was the natural selection for trail boss on Trail Drive '87, a re-creation of the old trail drive of horses from Stampede Ranch to Stampede Park that commemorated the 75th anniversary of the Stampede Rodeo, and Trail 2,000, held to recognize the millennium.

The all-around cowboy had done it all, and the Stampede was fortunate to have Pugh as an advisor and stock handler at the Rodeo and the Ranch until his passing in 2004 at 81 years of age.

## Caring for the broncs

Bucking horses love to buck — they've been bred to do so for generations, and they're good at it. When they're working, the horses buck for 8 seconds per go, for a total of about 120 seconds — 2 minutes of superstar athletic performance per season.

From the Stampede's stock of 450, less than half are chosen to perform at most 15 times per year. Sixty of them might travel 30 days a year to 10 rodeos. In wintertime, some of the herd's superstars — the A Team — perform at several high-profile rodeos in the United States, including San Antonio, Houston, and Denver. In the spring and summer, the horses stay close to the Ranch, performing at local rodeos, including their most important trip, to Calgary for the Stampede.

The rodeo manager selects the best bucking horses available, with each animal performing only once or twice, during the entire 10 days of Stampede. Fall finds a few of these bucking horses back in the northwestern United States performing at rodeos in Idaho, Oregon, and Washington. A few of these A Team horses will be selected, by the cowboys who compete on them, to perform at the Canadian Finals Rodeo in Edmonton in November and the National Finals Rodeo at Las Vegas in December.

For conditioning purposes, about six weeks prior to a big show, the Stampede bucking horses that have been selected to perform are taken off a grass diet and start to be fed oats and hay. For the last three weeks, they're put on a regimented exercise program to ensure they are in top condition.

Come rodeo time, standing in bedded pens with high-quality feed, these pampered athletes have only the best of care. The herd's health is carefully monitored, with regular veterinary checks, up-to-date vaccinations, and a farrier program that ensures the horses' feet are trimmed and

in the best shape. Between performances, they either return to the Ranch or go to another location to ensure they're comfortable and rested for their next turn to buck. Rodeo announcers can always tell Calgary Stampede stock because they look as good as they buck.

## "Born to Buck" breeding and embryo transplant program

The Calgary Stampede's breeding program makes an important contribution to the sport of rodeo in North America. Successfully predicting the mare and stallion crosses that will produce the best buckers, the Stampede consistently turns out rodeo stock that is considered among the best in the world.

Careful analysis of stallions' and mares' characteristics results in educated forecasts of the potential of particular breedings. One consideration, according to former ranch vet Donald Moore, is that the strongest tendency to buck seems to

### The Coconut Family

**Grated Coconut,** born in 1997, may be a half-tonne herd sire used to bucking off even the best cowboys, but to Robin Burwash, rodeo/ranch manager of the Calgary Stampede, he's just a big halter-broke pet who loves to be brushed.

Although Grated Coconut has a people-friendly personality not typical in a bucker, he's no slouch at his job. Short-backed, he breaks over so far in his bucking motion that his rump often hits riders in the back, knocking them forward. Grated Coconut competes at all the large rodeos, including the Stampede, Canadian Finals Rodeo, and National Finals Rodeo, and is a two-time Canadian and two-time world champion bucking horse — one cowboy says he's the definition of rank.

Naturally, the Stampede would like to see a whole bunch of coconuts like Grated Coconut. However, this coconut didn't just fall from the tree. His mother, Coconut Roll, performs alongside her son at all the top rodeos, including the Calgary Stampede, Canadian Finals, and National Finals Rodeo. His father, Wyatt Earp, was bucking horse of the National Finals Rodeo and his grandmother Rolly Polly and grandfather Wild Strawberry were great bucking horses in their own rights, competing at these same high-level rodeos.

**Above:** Bareback riding: the ultimate challenge of bronc and rider.

originate in the mare. The Stampede tries to improve those odds by using select stallions in its breeding program. Mares and stallions are selected and matched for size and conformation but ultimately the desire to buck is the final factor. A good match will be confirmed when a horse finally bucks at four years of age.

To ensure the continuation of, and to improve, the quality of bucking horses, the Stampede Ranch, in addition to traditional breeding practices, is experimenting with a state-of-the-art embryo transplant program. The Stampede's select bucking mares are bred to its top stallion, Grated Coconut, two-time world champion bucking horse. Once the embryo has established in the mare, eight days later, it is transferred to a surrogate mare to be carried to term. Every spring since 2004, the new crop of foals is anxiously awaited from the surrogate mothers, while the talented embryo donors continue to work the rodeo circuit.

The quality of the Ranch's bucking stock

has improved markedly over the years, with the Ranch producing more than 30 champion horses since its inception in 1961. Through its breeding program, the Stampede wants to ensure this legacy continues. Some horses have bucked for more than 20 years, including the famous Cindy Rocket, the former champion and queen of the Rocket line of bucking horses, who died in 1989 at the ripe old age of 28. The Coconut family is another group of well-known bucking horses on the Ranch's A Team.

## The making of a bronc

While perhaps only a third of all the Ranch's offspring develop into rodeo performers, the ones that do often become champions. Generally speaking, a young horse's bucking potential can't be determined for five years. In the meantime, the Ranch keeps performance records of each of its bucking horses throughout its career. This database becomes fairly extensive, with 450 head over 45 years of breeding.

At 4 years old, the young, unproven horses are auditioned or "dummied out" by ranch hands. Weighted dummies simulating riders test the young horses' bucking ability. The horses are usually halter-broke at this time, so they can be led outside the arena once a rider has dismounted. They're also "chute trained," which relaxes them in the bucking chute so they can save their explosive energy for the infield.

At 5 years of age, novice horses are entered in rodeos to determine their potential for the Stampede's bucking program. A horse that ducks, dives, and twists around the arena is marked higher than one that goes straight down the ring. Truly rank and stylish broncos buck high, with their hind legs reaching above their heads when their front feet hit the ground.

By the time the horses are 6, they are ready to rodeo in the big times. Though most horses' prime is from 6 to 12 years of age, the Stampede has many that perform well into their late teens and early 20s.

## Bulls

Although the Stampede Ranch is home to approximately 90 bucking bulls, the breeding program is quite different from the one designed for bucking horses. No cows are kept on site. Rather, the Ranch leases its bulls to local bull breeders then purchases promising progeny as yearlings from the breeders.

While horses can buck well into their 20s, a bull's career is generally winding down by the time he is 8. Since bulls don't hit their stride until they are 3 or 4 years old, it would take a huge herd for the Ranch to provide its entire requirement for bucking stock for the Stampede Rodeo. Breeding bulls to buck does, however, have a higher success rate than the bronc program — about half the bulls purchased are kept as rodeo stock. One of the Ranch's bulls was a world champion who remains a favourite with most who knew him — Outlaw.

### Stampede Ranch Champions

*SB = Saddle bronc, BB = Bareback

| HALL OF FAME INDUCTEES | | |
|---|---|---|
| Wanda Dee | SB | 1988 |
| Cindy Rocket | BB | 1993 |
| Moon Rocket | BB | 1997 |
| Lonesome Me | BB/SB | 2001 |
| Guilty Cat | BB | 2002 |
| **CANADIAN** | | |
| Red Wing | SB | 1961 |
| Zone Along | SB | 1973 |
| Moon Rocket | BB | 1976 |
| Guilty Cat | SB | 1982 |
| | BB | 1989 |
| Lonesome Me | BB | 1984 |
| | SB | 1990, 1991 |
| Kloud Grey | SB | 1987 |
| Papa Smurf | SB | 1988 |
| Grated Coconut | BB | 2003, 2004, 2005 |
| **CANADIAN FINALS RODEO** | | |
| Guilty Cat | SB | 1985 |
| Go Wild | SB | 1986 |
| Kloud Grey | SB | 1987 |
| Papa Smurf | SB | 1988 |
| Lonesome Me | SB | 1988, 1991 |
| Outlaw | (Bull) | 2002 |
| Grated Coconut | BB | 2004 |
| **World** | | |
| Wanda Dee | SB | 1964 |
| Moon Rocket | BB | 1976 |
| Lonesome Me | BB | 1984, 1994 |
| | SB | 1989, 1990 |
| Kloud Grey | SB | 1987 |
| Grated Coconut | BB | 2003 |
| **NATIONAL FINALS RODEO** | | |
| Cindy Rocket | BB | 1969 |
| Zone Along | SB | 1974 |
| Lonesome Me | BB | 1984 |
| River Bubbles | BB | 1993 |
| **CALGARY STAMPEDE** | | |
| Zone Along | SB | 1973 |
| Guilty Cat | SB | 1976, 1981, 1982 |
| | BB | 1987 |
| Arsenic | BB | 1979 |
| Blackout | SB | 1980, 1985 |
| Moon Rocket | BB | 1981 |
| Lonesome Me | BB | 1984, 1985, 1986, 1993 |
| Go Wild | SB | 1986, 1987 |
| Spirit Sings | SB | 1988 |
| Beetle Bailey | SB | 1989 |
| Controller | SB | 1991 |
| Grated Coconut | BB | 2002, 2005 |
| Gross Beetle | BB | 2003 |
| Outlaw | (Bull) | 2003 |
| **1988 WINTER OLYMPIC GAMES** | | |
| Kloud Grey | Gold SB | |
| Guilty Cat | Silver BB | |
| Lonesome Me | Bronze SB | |

**Above:** Outlaw, a 1,000 kilogram bull, showed his superstar qualities with every ride.

**Opposite:** The wild horse race is a wild test of the fittest, the most agile, and the most persistent — be they man or horse!

## A favourite Outlaw

Keith Marrington, senior manager of the Rodeo, has the usual family photographs on his desk, but most prominently displayed are two of the red and white spotted, 1,000-kilogram Outlaw, proudly pawing the ground beside a shiny red pickup. The champion bull won the truck as the bucking bull of the 2002 Canadian Finals Rodeo.

Marrington always recognized and respected this bull's distinct personality. Buying him as a calf, Marrington watched him develop into an intelligent superstar bucker with 40-centimetre horns. He normally spun left immediately out of the gate, but if a rider set a trap to be ready for the spin left, he would spin right instead. Robin Burwash was another fan. "He never hooked anyone in his life. He just didn't like to be ridden. The longer you stayed on, the harder he bucked."

Perhaps Outlaw's greatest moment of glory was at the 2004 Calgary Stampede, where he made history after throwing his rider, Steve Turner, with sensational style. The bell clanging on his bull rope signalled the closing of the New York Stock Exchange that day — and the opening of the Calgary Stampede Rodeo.

Despite Outlaw's legendary ability to throw off every cowboy but one (Justin Volz), the entire rodeo community mourned the "gentleman and athlete" when he passed away. He's buried in the hillside graveyard overlooking the entrance to the Calgary Stampede Ranch, but his red truck continues to honour his memory — as part of the rodeo sport medical support team's equipment.

# chapter six

# The Magic of Rodeo

## The origins of rodeo

To ease their transition to a new country and life, immigrants traditionally bring their old customs — including their favourite sports. The British and European pastimes of the hunt and polo joined the informal horse racing and other sports already enjoyed by native peoples in North America.

Mexican and American cowboys coming north to Canada brought their own horse-based cowboy games, which particularly helped cowboys transition to the new country and cowboy life in general. The roots of many of these recreational pursuits were based in the rituals of roundups and branding on the open range. In fact, "rodeo," from the Spanish word rodear, means to "gather" (cattle or horses to be counted and branded).

In the days when there were no fences to corral cattle and ranches were many kilometres apart, roundups were an important part of the cowboys' work and social life — and branding was an integral part of the economy of the cattle industry, ensuring that ownership could always be established. Ranches would work together on the roundups, with larger ones often sending the cooks and chuckwagons to feed all the cowboys. Groups of cowboys would be sent as far out as there were cattle to be found, and the cattle were herded to different campsites every night en route to their home ranches.

Riding into the herds on specially trained cutting and roping horses, the cowboys had to separate cattle according to their various brands and separate calves from their mothers to brand them. Calves were notoriously hard to chase, so cowboys honed their roping skills into an art form.

As well, wild mustangs had to be caught and broken for ranch work. Breaking broncs meant extra money for the cowboys and bragging rights: the ability to ride a bucking horse was admired as much then as now. "Never a horse that can't be rode; never a rider that can't be throwed" was the old range axiom.

Sometimes the roundups — held in spring and fall — could take months. In between, there were slow times, and it didn't take long before cowboys were turning their everyday chores into contests of skill. Early rodeo contests suited

## Cowboy Skills

**To be gainfully employed,** cowboys of the open-range era generally had to be tough, hardy, loyal, and skilled with horses, ropes, and branding irons. Horses had to be caught and broke to ride and cattle had to be corralled — tasks that weren't easy if you weren't born to them. Greenhorn Canadian cowboys — a mix of westerners, eastern farm boys, and overseas immigrants — may have adopted the cowboy heritage of the Mexican vaqueros and learned much from their American forerunners, but they had to adapt it all to uniquely western conditions such as glacier stream crossings during blizzards.

When the era of open-range ranching ended, cowboy culture lived on thanks to wild west shows, dime novels, and early silent movies. Wild west shows were a worldwide phenomenon, glamorizing the skills and aura of the cowboy through demonstrations and staged acts. At a time when the continent was becoming increasingly urbanized, the cowboy — a symbol of courage, independence, and mobility — became a romanticized and popularized icon.

As early as 1893, at his Bar U Ranch, George Lane (one of the future Big Four) was hosting his own exhibitions of what were called "interesting cowboy sports" — roping and riding tricks and bronc riding. The life of the cowboy was sometimes monotonous, always physically challenging, and perhaps lonely, requiring long weeks of work without breaks. Social events on ranches and spontaneous contests accompanying roundups were heartily welcomed, with the celebratory atmosphere urged on by bragging and betting. Breaking unbreakable horses and roping just about anything were routines of range life the cowboys knew well.

**Above:** In the chutes, the rider is ready for action and the ground crew prepares to release the gate.

the cowboys' lifestyle and honed their skills.

At first, the entertainer and the entertained were one and the same — the cowboys. As urban centres were established, these impromptu cowboy games gravitated to town, increasing their audience base. Rodeo evolved from these sporting rites. As rodeo became a professional sport, it still featured the signature skills of the ranch work that it originated from.

## How rodeo came to Calgary

Considered the heartland of rodeo in Canada, southern Alberta hosted rodeo-type events as early as 1893. George Lane of the Bar U Ranch south of Longview organized a steer roping contest and was beaten soundly by one of his employees, John Ware, who became one of the area's most respected ranchers.

The next year, Lane added bronc riding to the festivities. There were no set time limits for riding bucking stock: a cowboy rode the horse to a standstill or till he was bucked off — just as he would out on the range.

The first organized rodeo in southern Alberta was held in Raymond in 1902 as a ranch vs. ranch challenge. In 1905, Bill Pickett performed bulldogging, the forerunner of steer wrestling, as a grandstand attraction at the Calgary Exhibition. (His agent at the time was the young Guy Weadick, who would soon create the first Calgary Stampede, in 1912.)

By 1910, rodeo had become a popular and profitable way to celebrate the feats and skills of the cowboy, but usually as a side show or part of a wild west show. Rodeo contestants were often contracted performers. The pay for demonstrators was better than for cowboying, and it was easier work. Only a few Canadians were involved in the industry as professionals: the United States had more available cowboys and thus more touring wild west shows.

The first Calgary Stampede in 1912 focused on rodeo events since they were "the offspring of the cattle industry," according to Weadick. Some events were competitive facsimiles of routine chores on the modern ranch, such as rounding up livestock, but many were modified to suit the rodeo athlete and enthral spectators. Offering $20,000 in gold and attracting participants from the United States, Mexico, and across Canada, the 1912 Stampede instantly became the "richest and most ballyhooed contest in the history of ranch sports."

The first Stampede Rodeos had no chutes or corrals to reduce the inevitable delays of the competition. A horse was blindfolded, and its assigned rider climbed into the saddle from another horse in mid-field. When the blindfold was removed, the action began — and, as with George Lane's 1894 version of bronc riding, didn't end until the horse was ridden to a standstill or the rider was bucked off. There was no limit on bucking time until 1927, when a 10-second rule was established.

## The business of rodeo

By 1928, the success of the Calgary Stampede had stimulated an entire Canadian rodeo circuit as more Canadians were participating in and winning events. By the 1930s, like many other sports at the time, rodeo was becoming big business entertainment, cast more as an athletic contest than spectacle.

By the 1950s, rodeo was facing competition from other forms of entertainment on the Stampede grounds, but it has remained popular with both casual and serious fans, who know it can't be beat for vicarious thrills. Rodeo is a wild, fast, and serious sport for both the athlete and the animal, staying true to its heritage of "dust, denim, and scars." The fact that anything can happen in rodeo keeps everyone's interest.

To produce a complete entertainment

**Above:** The moment of truth in steer wrestling: the hazing horse on the steer's right keeps the steer running straight as the cowboy leaps from his horse.

package unique to the Calgary Stampede, former world champion saddle bronc rider and long-time Stampede Rodeo manager Winston Bruce added colourful opening and intermission acts, as well as music and pyrotechnics. Robin Burwash, the Rodeo's current manager, likes to give fans insights into what goes on behind the scenes of the thrilling action of competition. In interviews prepared for the television market, which are also shown on the large screens at the grandstand, sports medicine staff members talk about their profession, and cowboys relate what it feels like to get ready to ride horses such as Grated Coconut and then describe the actual rides.

## A league of its own

"Without rodeo, the Calgary festival would just be a country fair; without the rest of it, just another rodeo," suggests Robin Burwash. He knows that the heart of the Stampede is the Rodeo, because it's

where the world-famous organization all started — as part of Alberta's agricultural heritage. His mandate is to maintain this central role while introducing rodeo and western culture to the wider world.

"It's the best rodeo you're going to see" is the confident judgment of someone who knows — multi-time champion saddle bronc rider Rod Warren. "Calgary brings together the top horses and the top riders." Because of the money and high standards, the Stampede Rodeo is a favourite among cowboys and cowgirls everywhere.

The Calgary Stampede falls in the middle of a long season that starts in January and ends in December — but Calgary is the one they want to win. The keen competition, rich pay structure, and unprecedented way the city gets behind the 10-day event all solidify Calgary's place as a top test of the best cowboys and cowgirls in the world. The enormous audiences don't hurt either — there's room for more than 20,000 spectators to fill

**Above:** A saddle bronc rider is thrown back in his saddle. Standard equipment includes a pair of sturdy leather chaps worn over jeans.

**Overleaf:** A dramatic sequence of photographs shows the tension that accompanies a saddle bronc rider moments prior to the release of the gate — and his ultimate moment of truth.

grandstand and infield seats and crowd on the tarmac, close to the action.

The Stampede Rodeo offers prize money for the daily go-rounds and finals that totals $1 million. This Million Dollar Rodeo is the first and only regular-season rodeo to offer such substantial prize money. The Stampede also offers contestants a one-day bonus payoff — rodeo's richest hour — in the final afternoon, when winners in each event collect not the usual $50 or $5000, but membership in the club of $50,000 winners.

## Professional cowboys

Some 10,000 cowboys participate in North American rodeos. Most indulge their passion on a part-time basis, with only about a quarter of them able to afford making rodeo their year-round business. From fuel for trucks that haul horse trailers and provide living quarters, to airfare, accommodation, and entry fees, it's an expensive sport. Competitors

must earn their livings by placing well on the circuit.

Cowboys rodeo not just for the money but for the adrenaline rush. The excitement is real, never scripted. So is the risk. It's not a question of *if* you'll get injured — just when, and how badly. "If it moves or rotates, any body part is susceptible to injury," says Dexter Nelson, founder of the Canadian Pro Rodeo Sports Medicine Team. For the last couple of decades, members of this team have been patching up cowboys at the Stampede and offering advice on maintaining mobility and riding while injured with the least risk. Unlike in most other sports, broken bones don't always send competitors home. "If you're worried about getting hurt, you will be, and then rodeo's not the place for you," says Robin Burwash.

But most competitors know what they're in for. Rodeo tends to be in the blood — it's a rare cowboy who comes from a non-ranching and rodeo background. Often the men helping com-

**Bareback riders** Robin Burwash and Steve Dunham were not only long-time travelling partners and best friends, but also each other's toughest competition. No one was surprised when they both made the $50,000 finals the last day of the 1986 Stampede.

After the first round, Burwash had a 4-point lead. His next ride was on Coyote, a good bucker, so he expected a good score and was feeling pretty confident about the $50,000 bonus. Dunham was out first on the great Stampede horse Guilty Cat, and he scored 83. All Burwash had to do was get more than 79 to win, but instead he tied with Dunham. The rules state that competitors must ride again to break a tie. Fresh horses were brought out. Burwash rode Gunsmoke and Dunham rode Bottom Line: they tied again with 78 points each.

Cowboys are used to competing once a day, maybe twice. Never had these two competed four times in a row. Their fourth horses were put into the chutes. A tuckered-out Dunham rode Party Guy and scored a 76. All Burwash wanted to do was get on and off his horse, Six Shooter, and he did — with a 76. The crowd went wild.

The exhausted travelling partners considered the 16 rodeos left on their itinerary over the next 12 days. Dunham probably said it best. "I travelled with this guy day in and day out for the past few years and I knew he wasn't going to quit, and I knew I wasn't going to quit, so we decided to quit together."

This is the only time there have been co-champions at the Calgary Stampede.

**Top :** Robin Burwash
**Bottom :** Steve Dunham

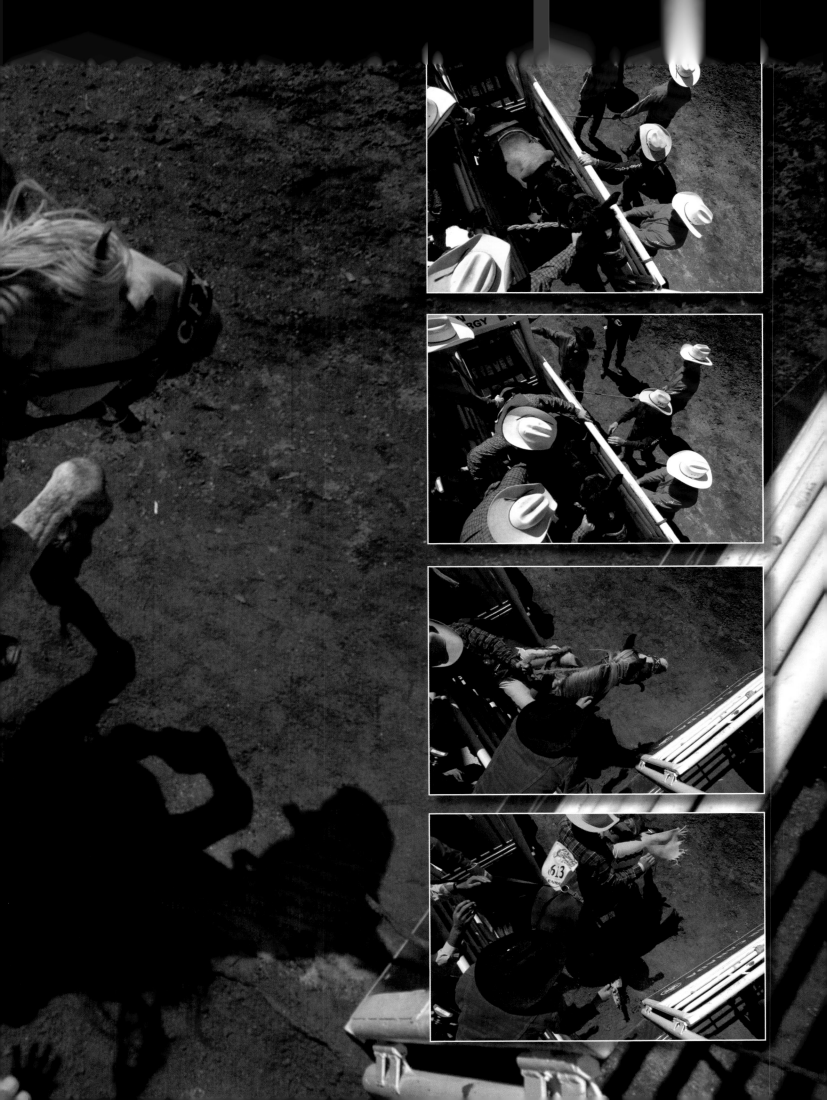

petitors in the chutes are their fathers or uncles.

Today's cowboys are working at a new level of skill development. Ranch chores used to be the first step in preparing for rodeo. Now, Little Britches, high school rodeo, and university-level competitions give young athletes the opportunity to develop their rodeo skills, just as other sports provide training grounds for aspiring players. Modern technologies, such as weight training and sports medicine, have also optimized athletic potential. "Although we see the athletes' skill levels going to new heights, I hope we never lose the horsemanship and cowboy instinct of working with the animal," says Burwash.

Despite the innovations, the rodeo community is still a relatively small world, not well understood by those outside it. Rodeo cowboys are as itinerant as in the old days, but they cover more territory. On the road for miles and months, often in motels or living out of vans, they often have only the companionship of the rodeo fraternity, which suits them just fine.

## Rodeo events

The events in the first rodeos comprised mainly the working activities of the ranch cowboys: riding bucking horses and roping steers, cows, and calves. As time went on, rodeo changed, expanding to include events that did not have roots in working cowboys' lives but that made for great competitions.

## Roughstock

In the roughstock or bucking events — saddle bronc riding, bareback riding, and bull riding — the goal of the animal has always been to throw the rider off. The goal of the rider is not only to stay on but to make it look easy and smooth. "It's a big challenge riding an animal that doesn't want to be ridden, that has no set pattern," says Winston Bruce, a former

## Canadian Pro Rodeo Sports Medicine Team

**Trailblazer Dale Butterwick** is one of those useful cowboys to have around the infield. In 1983, he had intended to help out his buddy Dexter Nelson as an athletic therapist for a year, but he's now supported or led the Canadian Pro Rodeo Sports Medicine Team on the rodeo circuit for more than two decades.

In the beginning, some cowboys didn't know what Butterwick and Nelson could do, nor did they want them around. Notorious for competing while injured, cowboys felt they had an image to maintain. Old-timers liked to claim that when they rode, "sport medicine came in a tin." That tin — of horse liniment — was all that kept rodeo warriors on the trail for months on end.

Eventually, the certified athletic therapists earned the cowboys' trust. Now there's no question that Butterwick, Nelson, and the rest of the sport med team are understood and welcomed. Professional rodeo athletes, as in any other sport, must take care of their bodies to maximize their performance. With coaches non-existent, cowboys have to take responsibility for their health and even learn to tape themselves. Butterwick and his team give them the information they need to assess when it's time to "cowboy up" and when it may be time to change the plan.

A researcher and teacher in the University of Calgary's faculty of kinesiology, Butterwick dreams of making rodeo safer and preventing injury. He's been working with professionals in the rodeo sports medicine field to create a plan to standardize the treatment of head injuries. If implemented, the next step will be research on the biomechanics of rodeo: investigating how injuries happen and how they can be prevented.

world saddle bronc champion.

Cowboys find it invaluable to get to know their opponents well — studying their tendencies and understanding their personalities can mean the difference between successful and unsuccessful rides. Things happen quickly once the chute gate is opened. A cowboy wants to be as prepared as he can for whatever the animal throws his way.

The **saddle bronc** competition dates back to when cowboys enhanced their pay packets by breaking wild horses. In the rodeo event, the cowboy hangs on to a thick halter rope with one hand and rides a saddle with a high cantle and pommel and stirrup leathers farther forward than usual.

Pete Knight became so famous as the most accomplished saddle bronc rider of the early 20th century, he was immortalized in paintings and songs. The most recent successor to the King of the Cowboys is multiple Canadian champion Rod Hay.

**Bareback** riding consistently produces some of the sport's wildest action. It used to be an exhibition event and another way cowboys could earn "mount money." They'd pull a loose rope like a noose around the horse's middle and hold on with both hands. Now, the bareback rigging is a wide piece of leather with a handhold like a suitcase handle. A cowboy is disqualified if he touches the horse or handhold with his free hand during his ride.

Some broncs will buck with a saddle or without, and some cowboys ride both ways, too. Herman Linder, Canada's Mr. Rodeo, won both events in his first Stampede in 1929, and then went on to win 22 more times between the two events over the next 10 years.

Clem Gardner was even more versatile. He rode broncs and bulls, roped calves, and drove chuckwagons, earning the all-around Canadian cowboy title in 1912.

"Are you ready for the **bull riding**?" the announcer demands at the end of the

**Above:** This action sequence shows bull riding at its best.

THROWING A STEER IN "BULL-DOGG
STAMPEDE AT CALGARY CAN.  OFFICIAL PHOTO
MARI

**Above:** A cowboy, fallen between horse and steer, struggles for a grip.

**Left:** Legendary cowboy Bill Pickett is credited with inventing bulldogging in the early 1900s when the steers in the competition were more mature than those used today.

**Opposite:** A cowboy and his horse demonstrate the true partnership of task and motion in the tie-down roping event.

Above: Bertha Blanchett, who was declared the winner in the ladies relay race in 1912, was a frequent rodeo competitor.

other rodeo events. The music intensifies and the spectators roar their assent.

The rules may be simple — stay on for eight seconds and don't slap the bull with your free hand — but, as they say, if it was easy, everyone would do it. Sometimes the bulls are such good contortionists, spinning and jumping more than a metre in the air, that they toss everyone off. Unlike broncs, which try to miss fallen riders, bulls will step on cowboys or hook them if given a chance, sending them flying. Rodeo bullfighters draw the bulls' attention from the cowboys on the ground, giving the cowboys

a chance to escape. The best bullfighters make this dangerous but critical function look easy.

## Timed events

**Tie-down** or **calf roping** is a practical skill still used in ranch work, but in the arena, the competition is against the clock. A successful go depends in large part on the roper's partnership with his horse. The cowboy must rope the calf, dismount, run down his rope to turn the calf over on its side, then tie three legs together with a knot that will last six seconds. His horse, watching every move, takes up any slack in the rope that would give the calf a chance to break free.

**Steer wrestling**, also known as **bull-dogging**, is for the biggest and strongest cowboys. The steer comes out of the chute at full speed, flanked by two riders and their horses. The cowboy on the steer's right keeps him running straight; the cowboy on the left is the competi-

## Linda One Spot

**Linda One Spot** has a place in the record book as the only female Stampede wild steer rider. As a 12-year-old from Tsuu T'ina, One Spot hid her gender and competed in the boy's wild steer riding event in 1952. She impressed the judges with three rides before her identity was discovered.

tor. Leaning off low from his galloping horse, he captures the steer's horns, leaps off his horse, and hits the dirt, slowing the steer's forward motion with the sheer force of his feet digging into the dirt. Using the steer's momentum, he turns its neck, flipping it on its side.

## The cowgirls

It wasn't just the men competing in rodeo. In the early 1900s, cowgirls travelled the circuit as well. In the 1912 Stampede, five cowgirls, including Flores LaDue (Mrs. Guy Weadick), rode bucking horses, competed in steer roping, and performed in the trick roping and riding events.

Although these queens of the rodeo were the first significant group of professional female athletes in North America and the first to be taken seriously by the public and media, participation of women in rodeo was rare, as in most sports of that era. Individual women contin-

ued to excel in their chosen events or contributed to the sport in other ways. Bertha Blanchett, for example, owned bucking stock, most famously Cyclone, who bucked off every one of the 129 men who tried to ride him, until Tom Three Persons stuck to him in the 1912 Stampede.

Although high school and all-girl rodeos offer a variety of events, professional women's participation has evolved to one event — barrel racing. Cowgirls and their talented horses enter the area at full gallop and run a cloverleaf pattern around three barrels before heading for the gate at top speed.

The Stampede considers barrel racing an equal partner with the other events, awarding the same prize money — the winner on day 10 goes home with $50,000 plus her go-round earnings.

**Above:** First seen at the 1912 Stampede, the wild horse race is a competition for 12 teams of three cowboys. Each team selects a horse from a moving herd, then ropes and saddles it. The winning team is the first to have both the rider and his mount cross the finish line.

**Previous Overleaf:** This photo sequence shows the speed and sheer beauty of barrel racing.

**Overleaf:** Chuckwagons and outriders thunder around the track.

## How the chuckwagons came to town

As Guy Weadick said himself, the Stampede was not "to be just an ordinary cowboy show," so in 1923, he created entirely new competitive events, including the "Cowboy's Chuck-Wagon Race." Weadick knew he needed a spectacular event to fill up the centre field and racetrack and wanted one that was western in heritage. He figured the informal friendly racing of the mobile kitchens during roundups on the range might be just the thing. Thus the concept of cowboys racing one another's wagons to town after long cattle drives was translated to a figure-eight start on a half-mile track. Outriders were added, and it became the only bona fide western Canadian sport.

The first chuckwagon race was a comedy of errors. Ranch owners were reluctant to risk their equipment and work horses for a spectacle, so Weadick had to bribe contestants from six ranches to partici-

pate. A character named Wildhorse Jack said he'd enter if there weren't too many rules. When the respected cowboy Clem Gardner was also recruited, the contest triggered the competitive juices between ranches.

In the first race, excited horses overturned one of the wagons. The outriders had to bury their faces in their horses' manes to protect themselves from the whips of the wilder drivers. The teams then had to simulate the setup of camp by producing smoke from a fire after they crossed the finish line. Chaos naturally ensued, but the first champion was Bill Somners, a Yukon stagecoach driver over 70 years old. For his record 2 minutes 50 seconds, he won $25 and a cowboy hat.

By 1933, the chucks had become more competitive, with drivers racing for bigger cash prizes. The challenge of setting up camp was eliminated in favour of an all-out run down the homestretch to the finish line. Over the years, equipment has been modified for the sake of speed and

safety, although it's still not light or easy to manage. Drivers also stripped down their wagons and replaced their work horses with thoroughbreds from the racetrack. By 1964, the total prize money was $30,000, but it was tarp sponsorship, starting in 1979, that made it financially worthwhile for drivers to purchase the best possible horses and equipment. Each year, proceeds from the tarp auction increase and add to the financial rewards offered by the substantial prize money structure.

Although chuckwagon racing has spread to other rodeos across North America, the Calgary Stampede remains the longest-running, richest, and most gruelling competition on the chuckwagon circuit. It's where the sport is king.

## Wildhorse Jack

**Pioneer rancher "Wildhorse"** Jack Morton used to hook unbroken horses to his ranch wagons after a roundup and race them to his house or the local saloon. Some say he was the one to suggest the race concept to Guy Weadick.

To win in the early races, teams had to re-create the setting up of camp. With no rules to stop him, Wildhorse Jack carried gas on his wagon. Instead of producing fire and smoke, the gas exploded, making his wild horses wilder. Wildhorse Jack was known for standing up and throwing his reins on the ground or pulling on his horses' tails, bellowing at them to run faster. Sometimes the horses were so wired, they wouldn't stop for a couple of turns around the track.

Weadick and the fans loved the showboating, and chuckwagon racing was a hit from the beginning, with a big thanks to Wildhorse Jack. He was also famous for being the first chuckwagon driver to do double duty, setting up downtown to serve flapjack breakfasts in the morning, then racing in the evening. Losing a wheel, breaking his leg, or ramming the heavy barrels all failed to stop Wildhorse Jack. He retired in 1938, when he was close to 60.

**Above left:** Troy Dorchester, a chuckwagon veteran, dashes for the finish.

**Above right:** The close proximity of horses, wagons, drivers and outriders make the chuckwagon races one of the most exciting events at the Stampede.

**Opposite:** A cowboy heads back to the chutes after completing his ride.

## "And they're off!"

Unlike for rodeo events, there are no schools that teach the sport of chuckwagon racing; however, many drivers are born to the tradition. Whole generations of Lauders, Glasses, Cosgroves, Dorchesters, and Sutherlands have grown up as "barn rats." Once they've learned the ropes, they enter the sport as rookies. Eventually, they move into the limelight of the Rangeland Derby, where the call of "And they're off!" sets their horses racing and the crowd's hearts beating every night.

Joe Carbury's famous call has started off "the chucks," as Calgarians and fans far and wide refer to them, since 1963.

"Hyaw!" respond 4 drivers, each with 4 horses per wagon and 4 outriders — 32 horses in total. They steer their teams and wagons around the barrels and thunder out onto the track to the roar of the crowd. It may appear to be a sport of impending calamity for spectators, but

it's a calculated 80-second game played by trained professionals who know what they're doing.

For each race, a driver must decide which horses will make up his team. His decision is always strategic, based on each horse's character and ability, the assigned barrel position, and the potential of the other outfits in the race. Athletic thoroughbreds with attitude hit more than 50 kilometres per hour in a race that is timed to 1/100 of a second, with judges to confer penalties.

Even the uninitiated in the audience join the tradition of betting loonies on each heat. Thousands of regular fans don't even sit down — they gather on the tarmac every night to cheer and socialize.

# chapter seven

# Agriculture

## The tradition of agricultural fairs

The activities of Stampede Agriculture are rooted in the earliest days of permanent settlement of the west. In August 1884, when Calgary was populated by only several hundred hardy, ambitious newcomers, the *Calgary Daily Herald* proposed that an agricultural exhibition be organized — area farmers were experiencing bountiful crops, and hopes for the future were high. In response, community leaders formed the Calgary and District Agricultural Society with the goal of founding a fall fair similar to the ones they had enjoyed in their former communities. Forging a partnership with Canadian Pacific Railway, the society sent a rail car housing an exhibit of grain and produce to eastern Canada to capture the attention of potential settlers.

After the success of the travelling exhibit, thoughts turned to holding a local fair in 1885. However, the region was unstable due to the Northwest Rebellion, so a second travelling display was organized.

By 1886, peace was restored. A modest fair held in mid-October set the stage for every exhibition that southern Alberta has enjoyed since. Volunteers from business, farming, and ranching organized every aspect, and prizes were offered for a variety of classes ranging from agricultural produce to home crafts.

After the 1888 Exhibition, the federal government sold 94 acres of land to the agricultural society with the stipulation that it never be sold or subdivided, or ownership would revert to the government. As planning for the fair progressed, the *Calgary Daily Herald* took the editorial position that "Farmers must remember that visiting strangers are sure to judge the capabilities of this country from what they see placed on exhibition at the forthcoming show, and if we are to secure a good number of new settlers from the visitors, the show must be a complete one."

By 1889, the Exhibition was still a relatively simple affair. Wagonloads of wheat were unloaded onto the ground for judges to look at, then sold, as farmers exchanged success stories and tips. Seven years later, in 1896, for a variety of reasons including a worldwide depression, the society failed for failure to maintain payments on its mortgage, and foreclosure on the fairgrounds was completed.

In 1899, a federally funded immigration campaign was delivering settlers by the trainload, and the fair was revived that same year in the form of the Inter-Western Pacific Exhibition Company. In 1901, ownership of the land passed to the city through a motion of council. The land was then leased back to the Exhibition. From then on, the fair continued to thrive as the city grew and ranching and farming activities in the area became solidly established.

By 1908, more than 25,000 people called Calgary home and the federal government granted the city the honour of hosting the government-sponsored Dominion Exhibition. An influx of grant money generated a surge of construction, which soon produced a gorgeous Industrial Building to display the fruits of the community's labours and new barns to house the increased numbers of animals entered in competitions.

## Staying true to the course

In the past few decades, there has been a significant change in the ratio of

**Above:** Heavy horses and their people take a break between competitions.

exhibitors to audience. In the not-so-recent past, half of Alberta's population lived in rural communities. Most came to the annual fair as producers, to exhibit their own products or to view their colleagues' successes.

But Alberta, like the rest of the continent, experienced rapid urbanization. Today, producers of agricultural products make up less than 2 percent of the province's population. "Agriculture is not a glorified lifestyle," says Teri McKinnon, a volunteer who married into fourth-generation pioneer stock. "Everyone admires the cowboys and the romance of western heritage, but there is little romance in mud, sweat, heat, rain, and the extreme of all of them."

Through all the changes, agriculture programming has remained a vital component of the Calgary Exhibition & Stampede. By supporting agriculture and staying abreast of industry advances, the Stampede plays a key role in the history of agriculture throughout southern

Alberta, as it has for well over a century.

And it all starts with the people. The model for the current volunteer-run Stampede was part of the organization from its infancy. Community-minded farmers, ranchers, and businessmen supported the concept and devoted their time to its success. Since then, numerous Stampede volunteers and staff members have come from Alberta's founding families of agriculture. Because of this, Stampede Agriculture has maintained strong roots while remaining an active participant in developing and supporting new technology that affects every sector in the diverse agriculture industry.

So although the fair, like the agriculture industry, is more complex and sophisticated nowadays, horses, cattle, sheep, pigs, poultry, seeds, and grains — the components of the early agricultural fairs — are still key components in the Stampede's agriculture programming.

## Celebrating agriculture today

At the heart of Alberta's history, the agriculture industry has continually evolved and adapted, and the 10-day fair has always celebrated the industry's contributions on a grand scale. Members of the agriculture community know how important it is to communicate with urban populations. Hundreds volunteer at the Stampede to ensure that their sector is well represented. This dedicated corps of volunteers provides the expertise of hundreds of individuals who represent an extraordinary pool of knowledge.

During the 10 days alone, 50 different agriculture programs take place on the Park, all of which have been planned, supported, and promoted by 22 committees and many more sub-committees, with the assistance of full-time staff. In addition, more than 1,000 exhibitors are actively involved, ensuring that the livestock and educational displays, which attract approximately 46 percent of all Stampede visitors, are of the highest quality.

For the farmers and ranchers, there are livestock exhibits, demonstrations, and competitions, while the World Championship Blacksmith Competition attracts competitors from across the globe. Other events offer entertainment value for spectators. Among the highlights are stock dog trials, cow horse events, and the spectacle of heavy horse hitches accompanied by symphony music by the Calgary Philharmonic Orchestra.

Sometimes the entertainment has educational value as well. It's been said that if it weren't for the Calgary Exhibition & Stampede, some young urban Calgarians would think milk and steaks come from a store. As the population has become more urban, the challenge for the agriculture industry has been to find ways to connect it to the rural sources of its food supply.

By providing a first-hand look at how the challenges of environmental and economic sustainability and consumer

**Above:** A team of heavy horses is put through its paces in the Big Top show ring.

The bull sale had its start at the turn of the last century and has been a fixture
at the Stampede for over 100 years.

**Since 1901,** hundreds of bulls have been prepared for auction every spring at the Calgary Bull Sale at Stampede Park. Limited to Alberta-raised bulls, it is the largest individual purebred cattle consignment sale in the world.

The first Alberta ranches raised Texas Longhorn cattle imported from the United States. It soon became apparent that to develop the new industry it was necessary to breed animals able to thrive in Alberta's vastly different weather conditions. Ranchers began the Calgary Bull Sale to showcase breeding programs producing cattle that could withstand sudden dramatic changes in temperature and feed.

Animals that demonstrated a healthy growth-to-rations-fed ratio ensured the best economic return for owners and investors. At first, Shorthorns were imported from eastern Canada to breed with existing herds. These animals were the high-selling bulls for many years. Eventually, the Hereford and Angus breeds were considered the hardy types that would offer the best return on investment. In the 1980s, exotic breeds from Europe, such as Charolais, Simmental, Salers, and Maine-Anjou, were added to the genetic pool of commercial cattle.

The Calgary Bull Sale has had a long tradition of being the benchmark for other bull sales across the prairies. Celebrating its 105th annual sale in 2005, the sale has kept more than a century's tradition of Alberta beef production alive and vital in the province. In line with the Stampede's goal to bring Alberta to the world, remote buyers have recently been able to participate in the sale through online bidding, expanding the market exponentially.

demand for healthy food products are met, the Stampede serves as a showcase for the agri-food industry. For example, BSE and avian flu have raised questions about levels about food safety and inspired greater curiosity. What is in the food? How is it produced — and is it safe to eat? The Stampede helps to answer these questions through its programs.

Ag-tivity in the City is another example of how the Stampede both entertains and informs. Starting as Stampede Country, which included such novelty events as log climbing and hypnotists, Ag-tivity in the City was introduced in 2004. To produce an authentic experience — while making learning about agriculture exciting — the Stampede formed partnerships with food and agricultural commodity groups. Now, tens of thousands of intrigued visitors take part in such unique experiences as driving a tractor simulator and milking a mechanical cow to touring a kitchen made entirely from crop residues. Industry-specific displays tell the stories of agriculture by-products: everything from crayons, lipstick, and Jell-O to heart valves and insulin. Innovations such as these are crucial to the industry's ongoing success and the Stampede's agriculture programming.

This programming isn't limited to those 10 days either. Throughout the year, the Stampede presents 10 other for

**Above:** Shorthorn bulls, introduced into Alberta over a century ago, were the best-selling breed for many years.

**Above:** Competitors at the world champion blacksmith competition work at their forge.

major agriculture events. Partnering with agriculture and livestock organizations, the Stampede produces events such as 4-H On Parade, the Calgary Bull Sale, and industry seminars focusing on agriculture and its importance to Alberta's economy.

## Supporting the western horse industry

Under the umbrella of the Western Performance Horse committee, S tampede Agriculture supports a number of competitions that have grown out of farming and ranching activities. A full slate of equine competitions, including reining, team cattle penning, and working cow horse, draws thousands of fans to the Park annually to celebrate the continued excellence of equine athletes and their riders.

The Western Performance Horse committee has been hosting cutting horse futurities and competitions for more than

25 years, first in the Big Top then, as the events' popularity increased, in the Corral.

The best horses and most accomplished riders in the country participate in Western Performance Horse events year round. Competitors come to Stampede Park for such events as Roughstock in the spring, the Stampede in July, and the country's largest cutting horse futurity in the fall. Competitors from all walks of life vie for championship titles in open, non-pro, and youth categories. They train their horses extensively to perform complex manoeuvres with the accuracy and precision required to take home top honours — in these events, the horses are the primary athletes. Watching a horse cut and keep a cow from returning to its herd is an experience not to be missed, an inspiring exhibition of the horse's athleticism and the partnership between horse and rider.

## The future of agriculture at the Stampede

The Stampede board of directors is committed to supporting and showcasing its agriculture roots. Its main challenges are effectively supporting a changing agriculture industry, connecting rural and urban communities, and keeping its agriculture activities relevant to the community. It does this by offering programs that entertain and educate as well as providing venues and support to a multitude of community partners.

As the global nature of agriculture increases and interest in agri-food information flourishes, the Stampede also plays a vital role in being a conduit between local farmers and the world stage. To support and encourage the industry, the Stampede facilitates fundraising and networking opportunities throughout the year by hosting such events as international congresses.

During the 10-day fair, the International Agriculture committee encourages worldwide business opportunities in agriculture by providing a venue in which agriculture stakeholders from around the globe can conduct business in a social environment. In 2005, the International Room played host to "Alberta's Advancing Agriculture," a showcase for a variety of agriculture products that included a hands-on opportunity to sample products and speak directly with their producers. This initiative provided an innovative opportunity for the International Agriculture committee to highlight product developments in Alberta's agri-food industry and assist fledgling companies in finding new export markets abroad.

As part of its long-term plan, the Stampede will invest in multiple, diverse, and dynamic ways to engage urban and rural audiences. Its ambitious goal is to help the agriculture industry connect with and educate consumers on food production, food safety, and the sustainability of land as a renewable resource.

**Above:** A new horseshoe is forged during the blacksmith competition.

**Overleaf left:** The excitement and hard work of competition claims one tired participant.

**Overleaf right:** Two youths lead their steers towards the arena.

## Youth and agriculture

**Knowing that support** for the next generation of agriculture professionals is fundamental to agriculture's growth and success, the Stampede supports and sponsors several youth programs. The organization's commitment to providing opportunities for youth to learn is one of the keystones of its agriculture program. Two major programs are 4-H On Parade, held in the spring, and the Youth Livestock Show, held during Stampede.

The 4-H movement in Alberta has a long, distinguished history as an apprenticeship program for rural youth, and the Calgary region boasts an enviable track record of long-lived clubs. Despite the reported steady migration away from farms, half the province's 10,000 4-H members go on to work in some part of the agriculture industry. 4-H offers public speaking experience, animal management training, and a variety of events that showcase the expertise and finesse members have acquired by working with their project animals. The Stampede's support of 4-H On Parade is fundamental to the cycle of learning

that occurs on hundreds of farms and acreages throughout the year, and the organization is proud of the role it has played over the years in keeping 4-H youth involved in agriculture.

The Youth Livestock Show promotes youth development, leadership, and entrepreneurship in agriculture by providing opportunities for advanced learning in areas such as public speaking, and livestock and industry knowledge. Competitors participate in dairy, beef, sheep, and heavy horse showmanship and conformation classes, as well as multi-judging and marketing competitions. These contestants experience new and exciting challenges that enhance their knowledge of the agriculture industry and all its components.

Continuing this commitment to youth education in agriculture is a focus of Stampede Agriculture's programming.

# chapter eight

# The Stampede in the Community

## Not just for 10 days

Since the establishment of the first fair in 1886, the organization now known as the Calgary Exhibition & Stampede has been at the core of community development. Its original goal was to showcase and celebrate the region's economy and lifestyle. Over the years, its mission has evolved to ensure that the organization preserves and promotes western heritage and values.

The Stampede's commitment to reflect and serve the needs of its community has not changed over its remarkable tenure, and although it is famous worldwide for its 10-day festival in July, the organization clearly has more to offer than its signature event. More than 2.5 million people visit the Park throughout the year, attending more than 1,000 events. More people visit Stampede Park for parties, concerts, grads, sports events, science fairs, consumer shows, meetings, and trade shows than they do for the 10-day festival itself. Generating hundreds of millions of dollars every year in economic value, through its own revenue and revenues brought to city and area businesses by tourists, the Stampede has proven to be a civic asset envied by other cities. It is a cultural icon locally, nationally, and internationally, its name and brand known in even the most remote corners of the world.

As a not-for-profit organization, the Stampede reinvests all revenue into its programs and facilities. As a result, it boasts southern Alberta's largest collection of exhibition facilities, sports venues, meeting halls, and barns on one site and is equipped to host hundreds of different kinds of events. The Roundup Centre, the key trade show facility, can be transformed from a car show to an agriculture show in less than 24 hours, demonstrating the sophistication of Park planning and operations. Peter Burgener, a Calgary architect and columnist who participates in Stampede team cattle penning competitions, notes, "The Stampede is many different things to many different people. It brings people together for business, cultural, and social exchanges in a reaffirmation of community values, despite [Calgary] being a big city."

In addition to hosting events such as trade and consumer shows, the Stampede supports both youth and volunteerism in the community through such established programs as the Young Canadians School of Performing Arts, Stampede Showband, and Stampede School. A partnership with Olds College provides a satellite campus for agriculture courses relevant to urban audiences. The charitable Calgary Stampede Foundation sponsors outreach programs, including the Youth Speech and Debate programs, and provides scholarships to young artists and agriculture students.

The Stampede has ambitious plans for its next decade of growth. Over the long term, it seeks to enhance its iconic status by increasing youth involvement, offering more educational opportunities in agriculture, supporting native heritage, and expanding its western theme in new facilities.

## The Young Canadians

Calgary never perceived itself to be a cowtown, aspiring instead to be a cosmopolitan centre. From the earliest days, entertainment was attracted to its vaudeville theatres and the annual Exhibition's evening show, which has been enthralling audiences for almost as long as Alberta has been a province. The heart and

**Above** The glamour of the Grandstand Show has been a symbol of the Calgary Stampede for decades.

**Opposite:**
The Young Canadians perform at the Grandstand Show every night during the Stampede.

soul of the modern Grandstand Show is the troupe of young singers and dancers called the Young Canadians. Their extraordinary story is typical of the Stampede's spirit of entrepreneurism and innovation, blending volunteers, theatrical arts, education, and commerce.

Peter Lougheed, a Stampede volunteer for many years before he became the premier of Alberta, was chairman of the Grandstand Attractions committee in 1964 when an experimental idea that "grew like Topsy" was conceived. Dr. Randy Avery, the Grandstand Show's producer, auditioned 300 local youngsters for 24 spots in the Calgary Kidettes, who performed on a one-time-only basis with the New York Rockettes. The audience's reaction to the Kidettes was so enthusiastic that the Stampede decided to expand the concept and train a group of dancers to be a regular part of the evening show — and an entertainment tradition was born.

In 1968, the troupe was christened the Young Canadians. At the time, the 90-minute Grandstand Show featured imported headliners — singers, comedians, and acrobats. The Young Canadians gradually replaced some of the guest acts. Singing songs such as "Up, Up and Away," the troupe underscored its trademark upbeat attitude, popular then and ever since with family audiences.

By the late 1970s, the Young Canadians had become the backbone of the Grandstand Show, no longer the supporting act. Over the years, the troupe has been an integral part of the Stampede's international profile, performing at other fairs and half-time shows for major sporting events in Canada, the United States, and Europe.

As the program evolved, the Young Canadians became a family business. In some families, there are two generations of performers: children have joined their parents to experience the magic of the Grandstand Show. Performers can audition as young as age 7, and some have

## The Young Canadians School of Performing Arts

**To perpetuate the success** of the Young Canadians, the Stampede set up a training facility in 1982 for its young performers. The professional training provided by the Young Canadians School of Performing Arts is one way the Stampede fulfils its desire to support youth and encourage such western values as discipline and hard work. Both Calgary school boards, recognizing the commitment the Young Canadians make to the program and to their school studies, grant high school credits to eligible students.

Dancers and singers aged 7 to 19 audition annually for the privilege of the free professional training covered by Stampede scholarships. Successful recruits are told up front that a lot is expected: performers must rise to professional performance levels by show time in July, and each year, that expectation is met.

The school operates 10 months of the year, and the senior and apprentice groups train almost year round in dancing, singing, and gymnastics. The junior troupe joins the action in late spring. The hours they put in vary according to their ages and specialties, but the time commitment increases as Stampede approaches. To gain performance experience, the Young Canadians perform at Christmas and at their spring concert, when students and choreographers have the opportunity to showcase their work individually. For most of the year, classes and rehearsals are held in spacious studios above the barns in the Agriculture Building, but in the months before Stampede, the production is moved to a hockey arena so the scale of the Grandstand Show can be accommodated.

The result of all the hard work and passion for performing is a special experience that, for many, is the highlight of their lives. Says Bill Avery, the producer and director of the Grandstand Show, "We try to create a place where individuals can find out what they can do on their own and what they can do collectively and how they can make a difference."

## The grand spectacle of the Evening Grandstand Show

**A million-dollar professional show** playing to a nightly audience of 20,000, this stage show may be fashioned in the grand style of Las Vegas, but it has one big difference — it's staged outdoors. In Calgary's variable weather, this is naturally a challenge: sliding while dancing in the rain and playing wet sheet music are rites of passage. But the show has always gone on, stopping only a few times in its long history because of lightning, gale-force winds, and torrents of rain.

A show on this grand scale requires the dedication of hundreds of people working for months behind the scenes to make it successful. As an example of the degree of planning that is needed, a fleet of taxis transports the Young Canadians to the Park each day during Stampede.

Such an ambitious effort also requires support from the community. In 2001, TransAlta sponsored the retrofitting of the mobile stage and the construction of underground dressing rooms to provide state-of-the-art production facilities. Now the show's design, showcasing a huge mobile stage pulled into place after the chuckwagon races end, can support even the most ambitious lighting rigs, special effects, and aerial acts, ensuring that the show's guests are as amazed at the spectacle as audiences were when the world came to their doorstep in the early 1900s.

stayed for 10 years, auditioning every year for their coveted positions. Some move on to the entertainment business full-time, some stay with the Stampede as staff and become teachers, and some just come back to enjoy the great show with the rest of the audience. There are more than 5,000 "old Young Canadians" alumni, part of Stampede's huge family.

The Young Canadians organization and Grandstand Show together are a family affair in another respect: first conceived by Randy Avery, the School of Performing Arts and the Grandstand Show are now directed by his son, Bill. Both masterminds in the art of producing entertaining spectacles, the Averys have created spectacular productions that draw worldwide acclaim. Each year's show is unique, but they all retain a connection to the past. Themes such as *Echoes of the Trail* and *Spirit of the West* salute Calgary's western heritage through music and dance numbers.

## Calgary Stampede Showband

The Calgary Stampede Showband was formed in 1971 as the Calgary Stampede's official musical ambassador. The first Stampede band had only 55 members and performed mostly at local parades and during Stampede time. The Showband has since tripled in size and, through international exposure, earned a reputation as the only two-time world champion of marching show bands.

Members of the Stampede Showband are between 16 and 21 and have successfully completed a competitive audition process. The young musicians and dancers of the Showband dedicate themselves to an 11-month rehearsal and performance schedule that closes with more than 100 appearances during the 10 days of Stampede.

The Showband's activities aren't limited to the grounds. Spreading the Stampede's western spirit, the band has participated in performance and competition tours of Canada, the United States, Europe, Australia, and Japan. The Showband boasts a résumé filled with high-profile performances for royalty and world leaders, and in military ceremonies and top-level world competitions. Its members are proud to have appeared in the prestigious Rose Bowl Parade on two occasions.

From its humble beginnings as a parade band, the group demonstrates its incredible advancement in its phenomenal presence and high-quality musicianship during field shows as well as in concert band, choral, and small ensemble performances. Members past and present agree that being a part of the Stampede Showband is a life-changing, unmatchable experience.

## Art at the Stampede

Art has been a popular feature of the Stampede ever since the first major travelling art exhibit came to the 1909 Exhibition from the National Gallery in Ottawa. The western art show at the first Stampede in 1912 featured well-known U.S. artists Ed Borein (who drew Stampede ads) and Charlie Russell. One of Russell's career highlights was selling 13 of the 20 works he brought to Stampede that year, which inspired him to start his famous North-West Mounted Police series. He also designed letterhead and posters for his friend Guy Weadick.

From 1931 to 1945, the art show was an annual event during Stampede time. In the 1950s, the Stampede provided the brand-new Glenbow Museum space for an annual exhibition. By the 1980s, the Western Art Show had become a regular component of Creative Living, now called Western Showcase. Winners of an annual judged art competition are awarded belt buckles.

The Calgary Stampede has long considered itself a patron of many arts, not only the juried art in Western Showcase. It helps raise the profile of all sorts of artisans' work through display and sales to the festival's huge and varied audience. It also invites chalk artists, card stackers, caricature sketchers, and temporary tattoo artists to its grounds as artistic entertainment. The walls of buildings across the Park proudly display larger-than-life murals based on historic photographs. Even the trophies the Stampede gives to its rodeo champions are sculpted works of art.

## Western Showcase

In the Roundup Centre, Western Showcase complements Stampede's Rodeo and agriculture activities by bringing western culture to hundreds of thousands of visitors. The Showcase grew out of a tradition of agricultural fairs. For decades, handicraft and culinary competitions and the comfort of social contact among farm women reduced the

Opposite: Members of the Stampede Showband

## Calgary Stampede Showriders

**In 1985,** the Calgary Exhibition & Stampede formed an all-female equestrian drill team to accompany the Stampede Showband. Riders between the ages of 14 and 21 rehearse 11 months of the year to ensure professional-calibre performances. In addition to acting as a colour guard for the Showband, the Showriders perform musical rides several times a day during Stampede time. They've become a well-respected, award-winning drill team with a distinctive western flair.

**Above:** The Palomino Room is filled with western art for the annual auction.

**Opposite:** Young cowboys await their turns at a fun-filled game on the midway.

isolation of rural life. In 1971, a group of former Stampede Queens and Princesses developed the competition and display formats of traditional fairs, creating the Women's World display, which evolved into Creative Living. In 1999, the area became known as Western Showcase.

Offering arguably the most diverse entertainment in the Park, Western Showcase reflects the broadest definition of "western." As it expands to feature more western-themed entertainment on the Window on the West stage alongside its popular Western Art Show, the showcase receives more exposure each year. On the Window on the West stage, singers, debaters, musicians, and cowboy poets entertain visitors with a mixture of old and new west. Kitchen Theatre, with its lineup of celebrity chefs, is always popular with audiences. The arts and crafts table has evolved into a much more comprehensive display, from artisans to the "make-it-and-take-it" craft section for aspiring artists. From jewellery to replica arrows to decorated purses or jeans, the Stampede Market continues the tradition of itinerant merchants.

## Stampede School

A project of the Calgary Stampede Foundation and part of the Campus Calgary/ Open Minds school program, Stampede School has offered students from grades

---

## Not your average art auction

**The Stampede's Western Art Auction** is not a typical sedate art sale. As befits the content of the art it is selling, the show is a lively western-style auction — but this gala event is only for art collectors prepared to bid high to take home their favourite pieces. Dressed in their best western clothes, guests enjoy the ambiance of the lovely Palomino Room as they look at the art on display and watch talented artists complete paintings or sculptures in under an hour as part of the Quick Draw challenge. A portion of the proceeds from the Quick Draw goes to the Stampede Foundation's art scholarship fund, which recognizes outstanding work by secondary-school students.

2 to 12 interactive learning at Stampede Park since 2002.

Teachers relocate their classrooms to the Agriculture Building for a week, and cowboys, historians, equine specialists, and other resource people ensure the students learn first-hand about western heritage. Students explore the past through such diverse activities as learning to saddle a horse, observing the cycle of grain growing and transportation in the Grain Academy, learning the basics of judging cattle at the Bull Sale, and exploring the gravestones of famous Calgarians in the Union Cemetery. Each experience encourages personal engagement and brings a sense of familiarity when the students return to the summer festival to enjoy the midway and other activities.

## The Calgary Stampede Foundation

**The Calgary Stampede Foundation** was formed in 1995 as a separate entity to be governed by its own board of directors. As a charitable organization, its purpose was to fund four core youth programs of the Calgary Stampede: the Young Canadians, the Calgary Stampede Showband and Showriders, 4-H On Parade, and Youth Speech and Debate.

Launched with seed money of $300,000 from the Calgary Exhibition & Stampede, the Foundation has since been financed with proceeds from a variety of fundraising events and charitable donations from corporations and individuals, including a Founding Donors campaign in 1996. Nat Christie, Harold Henker, Jerry D'Arcy, Ed Galvin Jr., and many other luminaries who were builders of the Stampede continue to contribute through donations and memorial bequests made in their names. One of the greatest supporters of the Foundation has been the Nat Christie Foundation, which gave six million dollars in 2004, to be directed toward youth programs and development.

Since its inception, the Foundation has expanded its mission to fund more than 30 youth programs and projects. In 2002, it launched Stampede School with a donation for that purpose from the Nat Christie Foundation.

The board comprises past presidents and other long-time Calgary Stampede volunteers and prominent community leaders from Calgary and the rural sector, as it has from the start. Under their leadership, the Calgary Stampede Foundation has expanded its reach well beyond the Stampede youth programs to support new and emerging youth programs in both urban and rural communities.

# chapter nine

# Stampede People

## Volunteers

For reasons that defy explanation, Calgary has more volunteer spirit than most large cities and is world-renowned for its entrepreneurial spirit and can-do attitude. There's no doubt that the Stampede's success lies in its volunteers' commitment and that their passion for making their community a better place to live spills out into other civic endeavours. Volunteers contribute to the hospitable atmosphere experienced throughout the city, not only during the Stampede but all year long. These people walk the talk of western values.

Calgarians' noble tradition of volunteering dates back well over 100 years. From the first Exhibition, in 1886, community-minded locals devoted their volunteer efforts to the fair's success. The model for participation they created has grown roots well beyond the Stampede. Now Calgary has the only international airport in the world where cheerful volunteers in white Stetsons greet visitors all year round. And where else but during Stampede can you have the province's premier or a company CEO flip your pancakes at a free breakfast?

When the Exhibition and Stampede first combined in 1923, the event was the biggest undertaking the city had seen to date, requiring hundreds of volunteers. The manager at the time, Ernie Richardson, created a network of people experienced in ranching and agriculture who could be counted on to lend a hand every year because they were passionate about their contributions to the fair. Founding fathers such as Colonel James Walker, A. E. Cross, and Pat Burns led the board of directors, joined by the heads of Calgary's most successful businesses, including a creamery, the stockyards, a bakery, and an insurance agency, among others.

As Stampede grows, so do its ranks of volunteers, who lend their expertise to more than 50 committees. Of these committees, 44 are responsible for activity areas such as Rodeo, Western Showcase, Youth Speech and Debate, and Grandstand Show. The remaining committees include areas of focus, such as Western Values, Governance, and Audit, and work directly with the board of directors.

Being invited to join a committee was — and still is — considered a privilege. The popularity of the volunteer program and the length of people's commitments has meant that it isn't always easy to find an opportunity to join one of the committees responsible for programs associated with the 10-day festival, as well as some year-round activities.

Typically, it takes six years for a volunteer to become fully engaged in the structure. After two years, a volunteer is eligible to become an associate, after two more years, a shareholder, and after two more years, a senior associate. Shares cost five dollars, have no par value, do not appreciate in value, and are not transferable. Shareholders are eligible to elect members of the board and to run for board positions themselves. They receive no monetary compensation but do enjoy a few perks, the most valued of which is the "badge," a pin that allows them access to Stampede Park and rush seating for the Rodeo and Grandstand Show.

The Stampede prides itself on its ability to attract and keep community leaders in its volunteer corps. Astonishingly, some of the approximately 2200 volunteers have earned 60-year service pins. Many have served 20 and even 40-plus years, and half have been with the Stampede more than 10 years. Even

**Above:** The Ranch girls watch the action from the fence.

those who become semi-retired after 10 years rarely stay out of the action long. Many continue to serve as the most enthusiastic greeters at the festival. They say it's hard to keep away once you've been bitten by the bug. They know they'd miss their friends and the camaraderie they enjoy in the volunteers' Wrangler's Roost in the Blue Room.

Few of the volunteers get much sleep during the 10-day festival. They work hard and they play hard too, enjoying everything up close and personal. Many book holiday time away from their jobs to volunteer at Stampede. This volunteer ethic reflects western attitudes about hard work and commitment. "Staying in the game until the job is done, and done well" is how *Calgary Herald* columnist Peter Burgener sees the attraction of being a good neighbour and volunteer.

Volunteers participate both for the tremendous sense of camaraderie they enjoy and for the feeling of ownership they get from being on the inside of this spirited organization. Stampede volunteers can get as much back as they put in — or more.

Teri McKinnon relates how joining the Stampede Agriculture Education committee helped her make the transition from city girl to farm and ranch wife. "I learn something new every day. I know this sounds cliché, but it could involve determining cattle weights, tracking grain

## Showdown

**An annual Showdown,** organized every June by Volunteer Services, kicks off the upcoming big 10 days. A signature Stampede event, Showdown sprang naturally from the spirit of the volunteers. Conceived and organized originally by the Queens' Alumni as an informal party called the Stomp, Showdown has evolved into a high-energy dinner-dance that volunteers look forward to every year.

Dressed in their best western attire, old friends and colleagues enjoy their annual reunion. Board members shake the hands of every volunteer entering the room, ratcheting up the event's incredible positive energy.

**Above:** Hangin' on for dear life during the wild pony race

deliveries, or any of the intricacies of operating a commercial feedlot. Some of those things might be second nature to someone raised on a farm, but there are times when I have to start from scratch with each new concept." McKinnon now happily passes along to others the benefits of her own unique educational opportunity.

## Exporting the spirit

Introducing western culture to potential visitors, immigrants, or investors is all part of the Stampede's mandate and passion — especially for members of the Promotion, Caravan, and Downtown Attractions committees.

Jack Hildebrandt, considered one of the Promotion committee's chief "batter boys," leads contingents of volunteers to numerous events all year round, flipping flapjacks while promoting western values. His replaced hip may be new, but the rest of him is over 80. Hildebrandt

is an official Stampede Life Member, and nobody does it better, say his team members.

The Promotion and Caravan committees often travel throughout small-town Alberta as part of Barnstorming and Bandwagon tours. They've also gone farther afield: twice, delegations have travelled to Hong Kong to promote the Stampede. Another group travelled to a Rolling Stones concert in Toronto to raise awareness of the cattle industry's concerns regarding the BSE crisis in the west.

## Who's in charge?

The structure of the board of directors calls for up to 32 directors. Twenty are elected by the shareholders from the volunteer system and 4 are appointed by municipal and provincial governments. A recent enhancement of the traditional structure makes it possible for a few community leaders to be appointed to

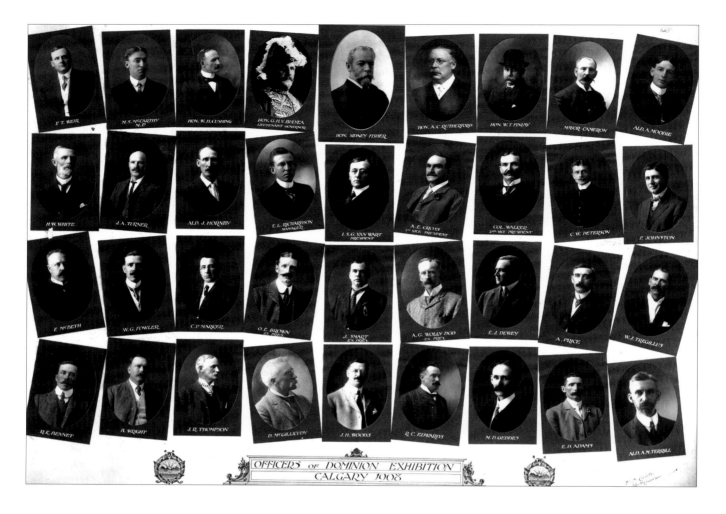

Above: The Board of Directors for the 1908 Dominion Exhibition.

the board, allowing the organization to draw in specialized expertise and networks to support its efforts.

It's not unusual for the president and chairman to have been a volunteer for decades before being elected by his or her fellow directors. The board carries the responsibility for ensuring that the organization is successful and relevant to the community. As stewards of an important civic asset that is known around the world for contributing to Calgary's strong sense of identity, the board has a significant responsibility to constantly renew the spirit of the Stampede.

## Royal ambassadors

The annual competition to find the Stampede's Queen and two Princesses began in 1946 with the appointment of Patsy (Rodgers) Henderson. The next year, a competition to select a royal trio was instituted as a charity fundraiser. Service clubs and community associations selected candidates and sold tickets to support their favourites: the candidate with the most tickets sold was named queen, and the two runners-up became her ladies-in-waiting.

## VIP treatment

**The Courtesy Car** committee provides one of the Stampede's most unique and popular services — community leaders celebrate Calgary and the Stampede with visiting VIPs, such as parade marshals, politicians, and entertainers, by chauffeuring them around the city. Imagine the surprise of the entertainer who arrived at the airport one parade morning to discover that his driver was former premier Peter Lougheed, who thought nothing about showing his guest the sights before parking the car and taking his place at the head of the parade as its marshal. Some visiting dignitaries have even been perplexed when it comes to thanking their hosts. Should they tip?

There's no question these VIP visitors experience Calgary's hospitality at its utmost. For their part, volunteers love seeing visitors' reactions to their hometown, exceeding all their expectations of this city on the western plains. Needless to say, positions on the Courtesy Car committee are much sought after.

The competition passed into the Stampede's hands in 1964. Since then, winners have been selected for their ability to act as ambassadors for the Stampede and Calgary, with emphasis on their skills as horsewomen. Candidates are judged at a number of events for their ability to speak in public and ride with confidence. Crowned at the Roughstock finals in the spring, the winners embark on a year filled with more than 400 public events at home and away.

The special bond that develops within this group of talented women is nurtured by participation in the Queens' Alumni committee, which assists charities by providing opportunities and western experiences to enrich the lives of special-needs children.

## Staff

Working alongside the army of volunteers is a corporate structure of staff members dedicated to fostering community spirit and ensuring the continued success of the Calgary Stampede. From 1923 to 1946, the organization operated with a modest staff of half a dozen. By 1989, more than 300 full-time staff were employed year round, 750 part-time year round, and 1600 seasonal staff were hired just for the 10 days of Stampede. In 2005, 3559 seasonal employees joined the 311 full-time and 1410 part-time year-round staff during the 10-day festival.

Many, such as Keith Marrington, have worked for the Stampede for decades. "It's a great place to be," he acknowledges with a friendly grin, regularly welcoming visitors to the Race Office. Dressed in jeans, looking more like a cowboy than a busy top-level manager, Marrington's not alone in his dress or attitude. Many of his colleagues have worked their whole lives for the Stampede, progressing through the organization as their skills and knowledge increased.

If they have grown up on ranches or farms, employees find that their work at the Stampede can maintain their strong connection to agriculture, the Stampede's lifeblood. Although Marrington now lives in the city, thanks to his work,

he's in touch daily with the traditional western way of life the Stampede is committed to honouring and preserving.

More recently hired, Robert Wise credits 4-H and the Stampede for keeping him involved in agriculture in his youth. He now works for the Stampede in the same building that housed his grandfather's racehorses. His colleague Max Fritz has worked at the Park for over two decades. Passionate about agriculture, he lives on a farm outside Calgary.

Every year, there are a myriad of details to put in place to ensure that the 10-day festival is successful. Each staff member has a trigger that says time is getting short until parade day arrives. For many, it's the start of construction of the Dream Home in March that begins the countdown.

The experience of working at the Greatest Outdoor Show on Earth is like no other. It's one thing to visit Stampede for a day or two as a guest, quite another to share one's workplace with 100,000 people every day. By Day 5, the notorious day when some employees and volunteers hit the wall, they often wonder how they'll get through the last half of this intense time. Fortunately their second wind is never far away, given the Park's intoxicating energy and the job's

---

## Retired royalty

**Unique among the west's** rodeo royalty, the Stampede Queens' Alumni Association was formed in 1971 and now includes women all over North America and Europe.

In its first year, the Stampede's only all-female committee helped with public relations and set up Women's World. Their first creation was a kitchen display in Flare Square that celebrated the past, present, and future. The next year, they took over the handicraft competition and display in a pink-and-white striped tent and produced professional fashion shows.

Since then, retired royalty have expanded their Stampede roles. Their association has overseen public participation games in Weadickville, driven tractors in a square dance at the Grandstand Show, and set up a display of images and memorabilia of past Stampede royalty. Since 1991, former royalty are most often seen in the parade; at the Giddy-Up Gala, their committee's fundraising event for the underprivileged; and in the Brand Room, as official hosts for the Stampede and its guests, a natural role given their experiences as Stampede Queens or Princesses.

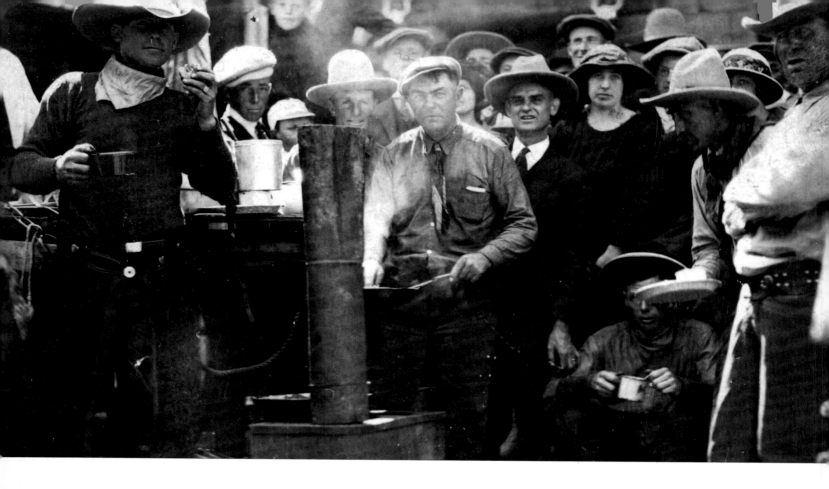

**Above:** An early version of the famous Stampede pancake breakfast.

**Opposite:** Patsy Rodgers Henderson was the first Stampede Queen in 1946.

immediacy. After the final day, there will be time to catch up on sleep and take holidays before starting on next year's plan.

For most staff members, the commitment to the organization's success continues 12 months of the year. They move seamlessly from their festival responsibilities to the hundreds of events that make Stampede Park a hub for continuing community activity.

## First Job

**For thousands of young Calgarians,** the annual Stampede means their first paying jobs and a treasured rite of passage to adulthood. Each spring, more than 3,000 seasonal workers are hired at the job fair. Many summer employees return to the Stampede to work year round in one of the many departments that offers part-time evening and weekend shifts, such as Catering.

The customer service training these young Calgarians receive prepares them to live the western values of hospitality and helpfulness. Working as ushers, servers, parking lot attendants, and cleaners, they absorb valuable life lessons and develop a customer-oriented work ethic that wil l stand them in good stead all their lives. And what's better than being able to slip out onto the midway after your shift has ended?

## The past becomes the future

Since its birth more than a century ago, the Calgary Exhibition & Stampede has remained true to its agricultural and entertainment heritage and has successfully balanced its commitments to these core activities. It has introduced urbanites to the wonders of agriculture and presented spectacular entertainment to both its rural and urban audiences.

The Stampede was built on principles that worked 100 years ago. Can it continue to thrive in a modern, urban, multicultural city of more than 1 million people? The organization's chief operating officer, Vern Kimball, believes the idea of the Stampede will live on in its enduring western values and its ability to combine its heritage with new and exciting programs.

It's the *spirit* of the Stampede that makes it possible for the 10-day festival to retain the magic of the past at the same time as it maintains its relevance in the present and develops its plan for the future.

Guy Weadick, the dreamer whose vision has borne fruit beyond his wildest imagination, would be proud.

# Hospitality at the Ranch
## Year-round recipes from the *Best of Bridge*

One of the values that has come down to us unchanged from the earliest days of western settlement is the community's support of its members, whatever the need might be. When ranches sprawled over hundreds of square kilometres of prairie, the rituals of branding the spring calves and rounding up the herd in the autumn were important social occasions focused on the very real need for neighbours to help one another.

Today, the seasonal cycle of ranching and farming has remained much the same, and good friends and neighbours work together as they did in the past. Hospitality is important on these occasions, and offering the most delicious food possible adds an atmosphere of celebration.

Since 1976, the "Best of Bridge" publishing phenomenon has helped cooks all over North America set a standard for hospitality that is second to none. This group of creative Calgary cooks has generously contributed a selection of recipes to *Celebrating the Calgary Exhibition & Stampede* so that the Stampede's tradition of western hospitality can be shared with the world.

These menus feature recipes that celebrate the cycle of the four seasons of ranching, from morning to night, using the very best in Alberta cuisine.

## Spring: Branding day

Before dawn on the spring roundup of cattle, what's required is a hearty breakfast at home. Lunch is a picnic at the branding site. And to celebrate a good day's work and an important task completed, dinner back at the ranch house has to include Alberta beefsteaks.

### A hearty breakfast

There's a busy day ahead, and this breakfast will get everyone off to a great start.

### Sensational sausage roll

| 1 package | frozen puff pastry | 400 g |
| 8 | slices bacon | 8 |
| 1/2 cup | onion, finely chopped | 125 mL |
| 2 cups | fresh mushrooms, finely chopped | 500 mL |
| 1 lb. | pork sausage meat | 500 g |
| 1 | medium tomato, sliced pepper to taste | 1 |
| 1 | egg, beaten | 1 |

Remove package of puff pastry from freezer 2 hours before cooking time. Cut a piece of brown paper to fit an edged cookie sheet. Poke paper with sharp knife to provide drainage holes. Fry bacon until crisp, then drain, cool, and crumble. Combine bacon, onion, and mushrooms in a large bowl. Add cold, uncooked sausage meat to bowl and mix well. Roll out puff pastry to edges of floured brown paper.

Preheat oven to 375°F (190°C). Spread the meat mixture down middle of the pastry. Place tomato slices all along the top and sprinkle with pepper. Cut the exposed pastry on each long side into strips 1" (2.5 cm) wide. (They should be about 3" [7 cm] deep.) Fold each end up over the filling, then lay the strips from each side alternately over the top to produce a braided effect. Brush pastry with beaten egg. Bake on brown paper "on rack" on cookie sheet for 1 1/4 hours. Serves 6.

### Tomato cheese bake

| 4 | large tomatoes, sliced salt and pepper to taste | 4 |
| 1/2 cup | mayonnaise | 125 mL |
| 6 | green onions, chopped | 6 |
| 1 cup | cheddar cheese, grated | 250 mL |
| 1 cup | mozzarella cheese, grated | 250 mL |

| 1–2 tsp. | Worcestershire sauce | 5–10 mL |
| 3 cups | *whole* milk | 750 mL |
| Dash | red pepper sauce (Tabasco) | Dash |
| 1/4 lb. | butter | 125 g |
| | Special K or cornflakes cereal | |

In a 9″ x 13″ (4-L) buttered glass baking dish, place 8 pieces of bread to cover dish entirely. Cover bread with slices of back bacon. Lay slices of cheddar cheese on top of bacon and then cover with slices of bread to make it like a sandwich. In a bowl, beat eggs, salt, and pepper. To the egg mixture add dry mustard, onion, green pepper, Worcestershire sauce, milk, and Tabasco. Pour over the sandwiches, cover, and let stand in fridge overnight. In morning, preheat oven to 350°F (180°C). Melt butter and pour over top. Cover with Special K or crushed cornflakes. Bake uncovered 1 hour. Let sit 10 minutes before serving. Serves 8.

## Lunch for the crew outside at the branding

These foods all pack and transport well, making it easy to take a break at the branding site.

### Muffuletta

| 1 | 10″ (25-cm) round Italian loaf | 1 |

Filling:

| 1/2 cup | pimiento-stuffed green olives | 125 mL |
| 1/2 cup | pitted black olives | 125 mL |
| 6 1/2 oz. jar | marinated artichokes, drained | 184 mL |
| 1 | garlic clove, minced | 1 |
| 1 tbsp. | minced jalapeño pepper | 15 mL |
| 1/3 cup | parsley, minced | 75 mL |
| 1/4 cup | olive oil | 50 mL |
| | | |
| 1/2 lb. | grilled chicken or salami, thinly sliced | 250 g |
| 1/2 lb. | provolone, mozzarella, or Swiss cheese, thinly sliced | 250 g |

Chop or process filling ingredients to a spreadable consistency. Cut loaf in half horizontally and remove enough of the bread to leave a 1/2″ (1-cm) shell. Spread bottom

Preheat oven to 350°F (180°C). In a shallow baking dish, arrange sliced tomatoes. Sprinkle with salt and pepper. Spread mayonnaise over tomatoes and top with chopped green onions. Cover with the two cheeses. Bake 25 minutes. Serves 6.

### Morning wife saver

| 16 | slices white bread, crusts removed | 16 |
| 16 | thin slices Canadian back bacon or ham | 16 |
| 16 | slices sharp cheddar cheese | 16 |
| 6 | eggs | 6 |
| 1/2 tsp. | salt | 2 mL |
| 1/2 tsp. | pepper | 2 mL |
| 1/2–1 tsp. | dry mustard | 2–5 mL |
| 1/4 cup | minced onion | 50 mL |
| 1/4 cup | green pepper, finely chopped | 50 mL |

of shell with half the filling, layer meat and cheese slices, then top with remaining filling. Press top of loaf on sandwich and wrap tightly in plastic wrap. Place something heavy (such as a dictionary) on top to compress sandwich and chill for several hours. Cut in wedges with a serrated knife. Serves 8–10.

| | | |
|---|---|---|
| 1 | red bell pepper, diced | 1 |
| 12 oz. can | kernel corn, drained | 341 mL |
| 1/3 cup | chopped red onion | 75 mL |
| 1 | jalapeño pepper, seeded and minced | 1 |

In medium bowl, whisk together oil and lime juice. Add cilantro, cumin, salt, and pepper and mix well. Stir in salad ingredients and correct seasoning. Serve at room temperature with muffuletta. Serves 6.

## Santa Fe salad

Dressing:

| | | |
|---|---|---|
| 1/4 cup | olive oil | 50 mL |
| 2 | juice of 2 limes | 2 |
| 1/4 cup | chopped cilantro | 50 mL |
| 1 tsp. | cumin | 5 mL |
| | salt and freshly ground pepper to taste | |

Salad:

| | | |
|---|---|---|
| 19 oz. can | black beans (turtle beans), rinsed and drained | 540 mL |

## Date-filled cookies

Filling:

| | | |
|---|---|---|
| 2 cups | finely chopped dates | 500 mL |
| 1 cup | water | 250 mL |
| 2 tbsp. | lemon juice | 30 mL |
| 1 tbsp. | sugar | 15 mL |

Cookie dough:

| | | |
|---|---|---|
| 2 cups | flour | 500 mL |
| 1 1/2 tsp. | baking soda | 7 mL |

## Skor bar cookies

| | | |
|---|---|---|
| 1 cup | margarine or butter | 250 mL |
| 3/4 cup | brown sugar | 175 mL |
| 1/2 cup | sugar | 125 mL |
| 1 | egg | 1 |
| 2 tbsp. | milk | 30 mL |
| 2 tsp. | vanilla | 10 mL |
| 1 3/4 cups | flour | 425 mL |
| 3/4 cup | rolled oats | 175 mL |
| 1 tsp. | baking soda | 5 mL |
| 1/4 tsp. | salt | 1 mL |
| | | |
| 4 | Skor bars or any crunchy toffee chocolate-coated bars, broken into small pieces | 4 |
| 1 cup | slivered almonds, toasted | 250 mL |

Preheat oven to 350°F (180°C). Cream margarine, sugars, egg, milk, and vanilla in large bowl. Beat until light and creamy. Combine flour, oats, baking soda, and salt. Add to creamed mixture and blend well. Stir in toffee bar pieces and almonds. Drop dough by teaspoonfuls on greased cookie sheet. (Leave room for spreading — the cookies, not you!) Bake 8 to 10 minutes, or until golden. Cool slightly, then remove to cooling rack.

| | | |
|---|---|---|
| 1 tsp. | salt | 5 mL |
| 2 cups | brown sugar | 500 mL |
| 6 cups | rolled oats | 1.5 L |
| 1 cup | vegetable oil | 250 mL |
| 7/8 cup | cold water | 220 mL |

To make filling:
Combine all ingredients in a saucepan and cook over medium heat until the dates are soft and mixture is spreadable. Stir constantly. Remove from heat and cool.

To make cookies:
Preheat oven to 350°F (180°C). Mix together flour, baking soda, and salt. Add brown sugar, oats, and oil. Combine well with fork, sprinkling with water and mixing to make soft but not sticky dough. Roll dough very thin. Cut out 2" (5-cm) circles with floured cookie cutter. Bake 5 to 7 minutes and cool. Spread cooled date filling on half of the cookies and place remaining cookies on top to form sandwiches. Makes about 6 dozen.

## Chocolate espresso cookies

| | | |
|---|---|---|
| 1 cup | flour | 250 mL |
| 1/2 cup | cocoa | 125 mL |
| 1/2 tsp. | salt | 2 mL |
| 1/4 tsp. | baking soda | 1 mL |
| 3 tbsp. | unsalted butter | 45 mL |
| 3 tbsp. | margarine | 45 mL |
| 1/2 cup + 2 tbsp. | sugar | 155 mL |
| 1/2 cup | brown sugar | 125 mL |
| 1 1/2 tbsp. | instant espresso powder or instant coffee powder | 22 mL |
| 1 tsp. | vanilla | 5 mL |
| 1 | egg white | 1 |

Sift flour, cocoa, salt, and baking soda in a small bowl. Beat butter and margarine until creamy. Add sugars, espresso powder, and vanilla and beat until blended. Mix in egg white. Add dry ingredients and beat just until blended. Knead until dough is smooth. Wrap dough in wax paper and refrigerate for 1 hour. Preheat oven to 350°F (180°C). Roll out dough to 1/4″ (0.5-cm) thickness on board sprinkled with icing sugar and cut in 2″ (5-cm) circles. Bake 10 to 12 minutes. Makes 3–4 dozen crisp cookies.

## Vanilas kiflei

| | | |
|---|---|---|
| 3/4 cup | unsalted butter, room temperature | 175 mL |
| 1/2 cup | sugar | 125 mL |
| 2 | egg yolks | 2 |
| 1 tsp. | vanilla | 5 mL |
| 2 cups | flour | 500 mL |
| | vanilla sugar to sprinkle | |
| 2 oz. | semisweet chocolate | 60 g |

Beat butter and sugar until light. Beat in yolks and vanilla. Gradually beat in flour and turn dough onto a counter. Knead until well combined. Form into a ball. Cover with a bowl and let stand for 2 hours. Preheat oven to 375°F (190°C). To make each cookie, shape 1 tbsp. (15 mL) of dough into a crescent. Place cookies on ungreased cookie sheet and bake 10 to 12 minutes (cookies will be white). Sprinkle with vanilla sugar and cool completely. Melt chocolate in top of double boiler or microwave. Dip tips of each cookie in chocolate and place on wax paper to set. Makes 2 to 2 1/2 dozen very professional-looking cookies.

## Citrus crisps

| | | |
|---|---|---|
| 1/2 cup | butter | 125 mL |
| 1 cup | sugar | 250 mL |
| 1 | egg | 1 |
| 1 tbsp. | grated lemon rind | 15 mL |
| 2 tbsp. | lemon juice | 30 mL |
| 2 cups | flour | 500 mL |
| 1/2 tsp. | salt | 2 mL |
| 1/2 tsp. | baking soda | 2 mL |
| 1/2 tsp. | ginger | 2 mL |
| | sugar to sprinkle | |

Cream together butter and sugar. Beat in egg, lemon rind, and juice. Combine flour, salt, baking soda, and ginger and gradually blend into creamed mixture. Shape into 2 logs 1 3/4″ (4.5 cm) in diameter. Wrap in waxed paper and refrigerate for 3 hours. Preheat oven to 375°F (190°C). Cut into slices 1/8″ (3 mm) thick. Place on greased cookie sheet about 2″ (5 cm) apart and sprinkle with sugar. Bake 6 to 8 minutes, until lightly browned around the edges. Cool before removing from pan. Store in loosely sealed container to maintain crispness.

## Dinner — back at the ranch house

Everyone will appreciate this reward for a job well done.

### Rib-eye steaks with grilled peppers and Gorgonzola butter (pictured above)

Gorgonzola butter:

| | | |
|---|---|---|
| 1/4 cup | crumbled Gorgonzola cheese | 50 mL |
| 2 tbsp. | butter, room temperature | 30 mL |

casionally. Heat barbecue to medium-high. Place steaks and peppers on grill. Sprinkle with salt and pepper. Grill steaks 5 minutes per side for medium-rare. Grill peppers until tender, about 10 minutes, turning occasionally. Transfer steaks to platter and surround with peppers. Top each steak with gorgonzola butter.

## Carmelized onion and potato flan

| | | |
|---|---|---|
| 2 tbsp. | butter | 30 mL |
| 2 | large onions, thinly sliced | 2 |
| 6–8 | medium baker potatoes, peeled and thinly sliced | 6–8 |
| | salt and freshly ground pepper to taste | |
| 1/2–3/4 lb. | Emmenthal or Gruyère cheese, grated | 250–375 g |

In large frying pan over medium heat, sauté onions in butter until deep golden brown, about 20 minutes. Cook slowly to caramelize. Preheat oven to 350°F (180°C). Grease a 9" x13" (4-L) or large round baking dish. Layer half the potato slices in a shingle fashion and season. Top with half the onions and Emmenthal. Repeat next layer, ending with cheese. Bake 50 minutes, or until potatoes are fork-tender. Cut in squares or wedges to serve. Serves 8.

| | | |
|---|---|---|
| 1 tbsp. | minced fresh marjoram or oregano | 15 mL |
| | pepper to taste | |

Marinade:

| | | |
|---|---|---|
| 1/2 cup | olive oil | 125 mL |
| 6 | large garlic cloves, minced | 6 |
| 2 tbsp. | minced fresh marjoram | 30 mL |
| 4 | rib-eye steaks, 1" (2.5 cm) thick | 4 |
| 2 | large red bell peppers, cut into 1 1/2" (4-cm) strips | 2 |
| 2 | large yellow bell peppers, cut into 1 1/2" (4-cm) strips | 2 |
| 2 | large green bell peppers, cut into 1 1/2" (4-cm) strips | 2 |
| | salt and ground pepper to taste | |

In small bowl, beat together Gorgonzola, butter, and marjoram. Season with pepper. Combine oil, garlic, and marjoram in shallow glass baking dish. Place steaks and peppers in marinade. Turn to coat. Let stand 2 hours at room temperature or overnight in refrigerator. Turn oc-

## Veggie stacks (pictured above)

| | | |
|---|---|---|
| 1/4" slice | eggplant or portobello mushroom | 1 cm |
| 1/4" slice | red onion | 1 cm |
| 1/4" slice | bocconcini cheese | 1 cm |
| 1/4" slice | fresh tomato | 1 cm |
| | grated Asiago cheese | |

Preheat oven to 375°F (190°C). Assemble stacks by layering one slice of eggplant, red onion, bocconcini, and tomato. Sprinkle with grated Asiago. If you prefer, replace eggplant with a slice of portobello mushroom. Place stacks on cookie sheet and bake about 20 minutes, until cheese melts and veggies soften.

## Frozen lemon puff

| | | |
|---|---|---|
| 5 | eggs (separate 3 and reserve whites) | 5 |
| 3/4 cup | fresh lemon juice | 175 mL |
| 1 cup | sugar | 250 mL |
| 2 cups | whipping cream | 500 mL |
| | vanilla wafers to cover bottom and sides of pan | |
| Dash | cream of tartar | Dash |
| 1/3 cup | icing sugar | 75 mL |

Whisk 2 eggs and 3 egg yolks, lemon juice, and sugar together in the top of a double boiler and cook until thick, stirring constantly. Cool. Whip the cream and fold into lemon mixture. Line sides and bottom of a 9″ (23-cm) springform pan with vanilla wafers. Pour lemon mixture into the pan. Beat the 3 egg whites until foamy. Add cream of tartar and icing sugar and beat until peaks are stiff. Spread on the lemon mixture and brown under the broiler. (Watch carefully!) Cover with foil, making sure it doesn't touch the meringue. Freeze at least 8 hours. Remove from freezer (taking foil off immediately) at least 1 1/2 hours before serving. Serves 10–12.

# Summer: Celebrating the Stampede

The most important celebration during summer is of course the Calgary Stampede. It provides a much-anticipated break from the routine of mending fences, putting up firewood, gardening, and tending to the stock. To prepare for a wild day, pick up a traditional flapjack meal from the back of a chuckwagon downtown or start off with a not-so-traditional breakfast. Lunch will be everyone's favourites on the midway — mini-doughnuts and corn dogs. A late dinner can be cooked on the barbecue if people can tear themselves away from the chuckwagon races and Grandstand Show.

## A not-quite-traditional Stampede breakfast

This breakfast may look familiar, but the flavours are unexpected.

## Cornmeal currant griddle cakes with apple cinnamon syrup (pictured above)

Syrup:

| | | |
|---|---|---|
| 2 cups | apple juice | 500 mL |
| 1/2 cup | apple jelly | 125 mL |
| 1 | 3″ (7.5-cm) cinnamon stick | 1 |

Griddle cakes:

| | | |
|---|---|---|
| 1 cup | flour | 250 mL |
| 1/2 cup | cornmeal | 125 mL |
| 3 tbsp. | sugar | 45 mL |
| 2 tsp. | baking powder | 10 mL |
| 1 tsp. | baking soda | 5 mL |
| Pinch | salt | Pinch |
| 1/3 cup | currants | 75 mL |
| 1 1/4 cups | plain yogurt | 310 mL |
| 2 | large eggs | 2 |
| 1/4 cup | melted butter | 50 mL |

To make syrup:

Put syrup ingredients in medium-sized saucepan and gently boil over medium-high heat for 20 minutes (watch

## Patio ribs (pictured on the left)

| | | |
|---|---|---|
| 4 lb. | pork back spareribs (3–4 racks) 2 kg | |
| 1/2 cup | hoisin sauce | 125 mL |
| 1/2 cup | oyster sauce | 125 mL |
| 3 tbsp. | hot chili sauce | 45 mL |
| 2 tbsp. | liquid honey | 30 mL |

Remove skin from underside of ribs (see Chef's tip). To tenderize ribs, slice each rack in half and add to large pot of boiling water. Boil gently until ribs are fork-tender, about 45 minutes. Drain. Stir hoisin sauce, oyster sauce, hot chili sauce, and honey together. Generously coat ribs with sauce on each side. When ready to barbecue, spray grill with oil and cook over medium heat, basting with sauce and turning often until well glazed, about 15 minutes. Serves 4.

Chef's tip:

To remove "fell" (tough membrane that covers bony underside of ribs), place ribs meaty-side down on a flat surface. Using point of a knife or your fingers, loosen skin and pull back along end of last rib. Grasp membrane with a paper towel or pliers and peel away. Discard.

carefully last 5 minutes). Reduce to 1 cup (250 mL).

To make griddle cakes:
Combine flour, cornmeal, sugar, baking powder, baking soda, and salt in large bowl. Stir currants into flour mixture. Mix yogurt and eggs in small bowl and stir into flour mixture. This is a very thick batter. Stir in butter. Heat lightly greased frying pan or griddle over low heat until hot. Pour batter in batches forming 3" (7.5-cm) cakes. Cook about 3 minutes on one side or until bubbles form and bottom is golden. Turn and cook other side until golden. Keep warm while cooking remaining cakes. Serve with warm syrup. Serves 4.

## Lunch

Everybody's favourite Stampede treats on the midway before the Rodeo — especially the little doughnuts …

### A barbecue back at the ranch

People can rest their tired feet as the meats cook slowly on the grill. The veggies are prepared ahead and ready to go when you need them

## Super-tender flank steak

| | | |
|---|---|---|
| 1 | flank steak | 1 |
| 1/3 cup | vegetable oil | 75 mL |
| 1/3 cup | red wine vinegar | 75 mL |
| 1/3 cup | *dark* soy sauce | 75 mL |

Slash edges of steak so they don't curl up under the broiler. Combine oil, vinegar, and soy sauce in a 9" x 13" (4-L) glass casserole. Put in steak, turn over, and marinate in fridge overnight, turning once or twice before you go to bed. To cook, remove from marinade. Place on broiler rack close to heat and broil for 4 minutes on each side (barbecued is even better — meat must be pink on inside). Place on cutting board and slice thinly on the diagonal from narrow end of the steak. Be sure to save pan drippings and juice for beef dip.

## Drumstick canapés

| 3 lb. | small chicken wings (about 15) | 1.5 kg |
|---|---|---|
| 1/2 cup | sugar | 125 mL |
| 3 tbsp. | cornstarch | 45 mL |
| 1/2 tsp. | salt | 2 mL |
| 1/2 tsp. | ground ginger | 2 mL |
| 1/4 tsp. | pepper | 1 mL |
| 2/3 cup | water | 150 mL |
| 1/3 cup | lemon juice | 75 mL |
| 1/4 cup | soy sauce | 50 mL |

Preheat oven to 400°F (200°C). Cut wings in half at joint. Discard tips. Place on broiler rack (or barbecue) and bake 15 minutes, turn and bake additional 15 minutes. Mix the sugar, cornstarch, salt, ginger, and pepper. Add liquids. Cook, stirring constantly, over medium heat until mixture thickens. Boil 2 minutes. Brush over wings. Continue baking or grilling at 400° (200°C) for about 35 minutes. During baking, brush soy mixture on wings frequently. Serve in chafing dish. Serves 6–8.

## Speedy baked beans

| 28 oz. can | pork and beans in tomato sauce | 796 mL |
|---|---|---|
| 1/4 cup | brown sugar, packed | 50 mL |
| 1/4 cup | ketchup | 50 mL |
| 3 tbsp. | frozen orange juice concentrate | 45 mL |
| 1 tbsp. | diced minced onion | 15 mL |
| 1 tbsp. | Worcestershire sauce | 15 mL |
| | salt and pepper to taste | |
| 1 tsp. | dry mustard | 5 mL |

Preheat oven to 350°F (180°C). Place all ingredients in 2-quart [2-L] casserole. Mix well. Bake 35 to 40 minutes, or heat thoroughly on stove top or microwave. Serves 4.

## Killer cole slaw

Salad:

| 1/2 | cabbage, chopped | 1/2 |
|---|---|---|
| 5 | stalks green onions, chopped | 5 |
| 1/4 cup | slivered almonds | 50 mL |
| 1/4 cup | sunflower seeds, toasted (or sesame seeds) | 50 mL |
| 1 pkg. | Japanese noodle soup mix, crushed (Ichiban) | 1 pkg. |

Dressing:

| 1/4 cup | rice (or white) vinegar | 50 mL |
|---|---|---|
| 1/4 cup | salad oil | 50 mL |
| | seasoning package from noodles | |

Combine all salad ingredients except noodles. Before serving, toss with the dressing. Add noodles and toss again. Serves 6.

## Super chocolate cake

| 1 cup | sugar | 250 mL |
|---|---|---|
| 3 tbsp. | butter, room temperature | 45 mL |
| 1 | egg, beaten | |
| 1/2 cup | cocoa, fill with boiling water to make 1 cup (250 mL) liquid | 125 mL |
| 1/2 tsp. | baking soda | 2 mL |
| 1/2 cup | boiling water | 125 mL |
| 1 cup | flour | 250 mL |
| 1 tsp. | baking powder | 5 mL |

Preheat oven to 350°F (180°C). Cream together sugar and butter; add egg and cocoa liquid. Mix soda and boiling water. Add this, flour, and baking powder, mix well. Pour into greased 9″ (23-cm) square pan (the batter will be thin). Bake 30 minutes, or until a toothpick inserted in centre comes out clean. (This cake doubles well. Bake in a 9″ x 13″ (4-L) pan or a Bundt pan for 40 to 50 minutes.)

## Autumn: A day to sort the herd

Back at the ranch in the autumn, it's time to sort the herd into those ready for market and others moving to the winter pasture. Feeding all the hungry helpers is easiest done out of the ranch house.

## Breakfast

Keep hunger away during the long morning ahead.

### Scotty's nest eggs

Each nest:

| | | |
|---|---|---|
| 2–3 | thin slices black forest ham | 2–3 |
| 1 | egg | 1 |
| 1 tbsp. | cream | 15 mL |
| 1 heaping tbsp. | grated Swiss cheese | 22 mL |
| Sprinkle | basil | Sprinkle |
| 1/2 | English muffin | 1/2 |

Preheat oven to 350°F (180°C). Grease large muffin tins. (Place water in any unused muffin cups to prevent damage.) Line with ham and break egg over top. Add cream and sprinkle with cheese and basil. Bake 12 to 15 minutes. Serve on half a toasted English muffin.

### Roasted orange pepper and corn salsa

| | | |
|---|---|---|
| 3 | yellow peppers, halved and seeded | 3 |
| 1/2 cup | chicken broth | 125 mL |
| 1/2 tsp. | cumin | 2 mL |
| | salt and pepper to taste | |
| 19 oz. can | kernel corn | 540 mL |
| 1/4–1/2 tsp. | hot red pepper flakes | 1–2 mL |

Place pepper halves cut side down on a cookie sheet. Broil until skins are blackened and puffed. Leave skins on and place in saucepan, add chicken broth, and cook uncovered 10 minutes. Purée with cumin, salt, and pepper. Add corn and pepper flakes. Store in refrigerator. Makes 2 cups (250 mL).

### Citrus cream pull-aparts

| | | |
|---|---|---|
| 1 lb. | frozen dinner roll dough or | 500 g |
| 1 lb. | loaf frozen bread dough | 500 g |
| 1/2 cup | dried cranberries | 125 mL |
| 1/2 cup | dried apricots, chopped | 125 mL |
| 2 tbsp. | butter, melted | 30 mL |
| 1/2 cup | sugar | 125 mL |
| 1/2 cup | cream cheese, softened | 125 mL |
| 1 tbsp. | grated lemon zest | 15 mL |
| 1 tbsp. | grated orange zest | 15 mL |
| 2 tbsp. | orange juice | 30 mL |
| 2 tbsp. | fresh lemon juice | 30 mL |
| 1 cup | icing sugar | 250 mL |

Thaw dinner roll dough at room temperature for 30 minutes. Cut rolls in half. OR Thaw frozen bread dough at room temperature for 30 minutes. Cut loaf in half and cut each half into 12 pieces. Place half the rolls in greased 2-quart (2-L) Bundt pan. Sprinkle rolls with half the cranberries and apricots. Add remaining rolls. Brush rolls with butter and sprinkle on remaining cranberries and apricots. Cover with clean tea towel and let rise for

30 minutes. Cream sugar and cream cheese together. Add lemon zest, orange zest, and juice to creamed mixture and beat until smooth. Pour over rolls. Cover with plastic wrap and leave on counter overnight. In the morning, preheat oven to 350°F (180°C) and bake rolls for 40 minutes, checking the last 10 minutes. Cover loosely with foil if buns become too brown. Cool 15 minutes. Place plate over pan and invert. Combine lemon juice and icing sugar. Drizzle over rolls. Pull apart to serve. Serves 8.

## Lunch

This hearty meal will warm up a cool fall day.

### Red pepper soup

| | | |
|---|---|---|
| 4 | large red peppers, halved and seeded | 4 |
| 2 tbsp. | butter or margarine | 30 mL |
| 1 | large red onion, chopped | 1 |
| 2 | garlic cloves, minced | 2 |
| 4 cups | chicken broth | 1 L |
| 1 tbsp. | lemon juice or gin | 15 mL |
| | salt to taste | |
| 1/2 tsp. | ground pepper | 2 mL |
| | fresh sweet basil for garnish | |

Place pepper halves cut side down on a cookie sheet. Broil until skins are blackened and puffed. Remove from sheet and place in a plastic bag to steam. Sauté onions and garlic in butter until soft. Remove cooled peppers from bag and peel off skins. Cut into chunks and add to onions and garlic. Cook for 2 to 3 minutes. Add broth, cover, and simmer 20 minutes. Add lemon juice or gin. In a blender or food processor, whirl 1/3 of the mixture at a time until smooth. (Strain if you wish.) Season with salt and pepper. Garnish with basil. Serves 4–6.

### Pâté en baguette

Pâté:

| | | |
|---|---|---|
| 1 lb. | farmer, Polish, or summer sausage, casings removed | 500 g |
| 1/4 cup | butter, room temperature | 50 mL |
| 4 | green onions, chopped | 4 |
| 3 tbsp. | sour cream | 45 mL |
| 2 tbsp. | Dijon mustard | 30 mL |
| 1 tbsp. | lemon juice | 15 mL |
| 1 tbsp. | prepared horseradish | 15 mL |
| 1 | shallot, cut up | 1 |
| 1/2 tsp. | freshly ground pepper | 2 mL |
| 1/4 tsp. | hot pepper sauce | 1 mL |
| 1/4 cup | fresh chopped parsley | 50 mL |
| 1/2 tsp. | dried basil | 2 mL |
| 1 | 24″ (60-cm)baguette | 1 |

Mustard horseradish sauce:

| | | |
|---|---|---|
| 3/4 cup | mayonnaise | 175 mL |
| 1 heaping tbsp. | Dijon mustard | 22 mL |
| 1 tbsp. | coarse-grained mustard | 15 mL |
| 1/2 tsp. | prepared horseradish | 2 mL |
| 1/2 tsp. | dry mustard | 2 mL |
| 1/2 tsp. | white wine vinegar | 2 mL |
| 1/4 tsp. | hot pepper sauce | 1 mL |
| 1/4 tsp. | Worcestershire sauce | 1 mL |
| | fresh parsley for garnish | |

To make pâté:
Finely chop sausage in food processor. Set aside in a bowl. Add next 11 ingredients to processor, one at a time, blending after each addition, then add to meat mixture. This will have a pâté-like texture. Remove ends from baguette and cut bread into 6″ (15-cm) sections. Using a sharp bread knife, hollow out the centre of each baguette, leaving a 1/2″ (1-cm) crust. Pack pâté into hollowed baguettes, wrap tightly in foil, and refrigerate for up to 24 hours, or freeze.

To make sauce:
Combine all ingredients. Cover and chill overnight.

To serve:
Cut baguettes into 1/2″ (1-cm) slices and serve at room temperature with sauce, radishes, gherkins, and olives.

dry mustard. Add vinegar and water and cook slowly until thickened. Remove from heat and stir in mayonnaise. Cool.

To make salad:
Marinate broccoli in dressing for several hours. Add remaining ingredients and toss well. Serves 6.

## Oven-fried chicken (pictured on the left)

Seasoned flour:

| | | |
|---|---|---|
| 1 1/2 cups | flour | 375 mL |
| 1 tbsp. | paprika | 15 mL |
| 4 tsp. | dry mustard | 20 mL |
| | salt and pepper to taste | |
| | chicken pieces, as needed | |
| 1/4 cup | margarine | 50 mL |

Combine seasoned flour ingredients and store in a jar. Preheat oven to 400°F (200°C). Place required amount of dry mixture in a paper bag, add chicken, and shake dem bones. Melt margarine in baking pan. Place chicken in pan and bake 20 minutes. Turn and bake another 20 minutes, or until golden brown.

## Broccoli mandarin salad

Dressing:

| | | |
|---|---|---|
| 2 | eggs | 2 |
| 1/2 cup | sugar | 125 mL |
| 1 tsp. | cornstarch | 5 mL |
| 1 tsp. | dry mustard | 5 mL |
| 1/4 cup | white wine vinegar | 50 mL |
| 1/4 cup | water | 50 mL |
| 1/2 cup | mayonnaise | 125 mL |

Salad:

| | | |
|---|---|---|
| 4 cups | fresh broccoli florets | 1 L |
| 1/2 cup | raisins | 125 mL |
| 8 | slices bacon, cooked and chopped | 8 |
| 2 cups | sliced fresh mushrooms | 500 mL |
| 1/2 cup | slivered toasted almonds | 125 mL |
| 10 oz. can | mandarin oranges, drained | 284 mL |
| 1/2 | red onion, sliced | 1/2 |

To make dressing:
In a saucepan, whisk together eggs, sugar, cornstarch, and

## Oatmeal crispies

| | | |
|---|---|---|
| 1 cup | butter, softened | 250 mL |
| 1/2 cup | sugar | 125 mL |
| 1 cup | flour | 250 mL |
| 1 1/2 cups | rolled oats | 375 mL |
| | icing sugar | |

Preheat oven to 350°F (180°C). In large bowl, beat butter and sugar together until creamy. Combine flour and rolled oats. Mix into creamed mixture. Shape dough into medium-sized balls and place about 3" (7.5 cm) apart on cookie sheets. Flatten with fork dipped in water. Bake for 10 minutes. Cool before removing from cookie sheets. When completely cool, generously dust with icing sugar. Makes 3 dozen cookies.

# Hospitality at the Ranch

## Dinner

After a long day outdoors, tired crew members will appreciate the flavours of this delicious meal.

### Marinated barbecued lamb

| 1 cup | dry red wine | 250 mL |
|---|---|---|
| 1/2 cup | olive oil | 125 mL |
| 2–3 cloves | garlic, minced | 2–3 |
| 1 tsp. | oregano | 5 mL |
| 1 tsp. | thyme | 5 mL |
| 1 tsp. | parsley | 5 mL |
| 1/2 tsp. | pepper, coarsely ground | 2 mL |
| 1/2 tsp. | salt | 2 mL |
| | juice of 1 lemon | |
| 1 | deboned leg of lamb | 1 |

Mix all ingredients together. Pour over lamb, cover, and marinate in fridge for 24 hours. Turn occasionally. Cook lamb close to coals for 5 minutes on each side to brown, then raise and finish cooking more slowly to desired doneness. Baste frequently with remaining marinade.

## Butter-baked taters

| 1/4 cup | butter | 50 mL |
|---|---|---|
| 3 tbsp. | green onion, finely chopped | 45 mL |
| 3 | large potatoes, peeled | 3 |
| | salt and pepper to taste | |
| 2 tbsp. | grated Parmesan cheese | 30 mL |

Preheat oven to 500°F (260°C). Melt butter in a saucepan. Add onion to butter and sauté until tender. Halve potatoes lengthwise, then slice crosswise into slices 1/8" (3 mm) thick. Immediately line up in buttered 9" x 13" (4-L) baking pan with slices overlapping. Pour butter mixture over potatoes. Season with salt and pepper. Bake 20 minutes. Remove from oven and sprinkle with Parmesan cheese. Bake an additional 5 to 7 minutes, or until cheese is slightly browned and melted. Serves 4.

Variation: Some like 'em hot!

| 1 cup | grated cheddar cheese | 250 mL |
|---|---|---|
| 1 cup | cornflakes, crushed | 250 mL |
| 1 tsp. | cayenne pepper | 5 mL |

Combine all ingredients. Sprinkle over buttered potatoes and bake at 400°F (200°C) for 30 minutes, omitting the Parmesan cheese.

## Tomatoes Florentine

| | | |
|---|---|---|
| 6 | fairly firm tomatoes | 6 |
| 12 oz. | frozen chopped spinach | 360 g (pkg) |
| 1 tbsp. | instant minced onion | 15 mL |
| 1 tsp. | garlic salt | 5 mL |
| 1 tsp. | oregano | 5 mL |
| Dash | nutmeg | Dash |
| 1 cup | grated cheese (Velveeta or cheddar) Parmesan cheese | 250 mL |

Preheat oven to 350°F (180°C). Slice top of tomatoes and scoop out insides. Chop and drain the pulp. Heat the spinach without water and drain well. Combine spinach, pulp, onion, spices, and grated cheese. Fill tomatoes and top with Parmesan and bake 20 to 30 minutes. Serves 6.

## Almond plum tart (pictured on the left)

| | | |
|---|---|---|
| 1 1/4 cups | flour | 310 mL |
| 1 tbsp. | icing sugar | 15 mL |
| Pinch | salt | Pinch |
| 1/2 cup | butter, cut into small pieces | 125 mL |
| 1 | egg yolk | 1 |
| 2 tbsp. | ice water | 30 mL |
| 1 1/2 cups | chopped almonds | 375 mL |
| 3/4 cup | sugar | 175 mL |
| 1/4 cup | butter, room temperature | 50 mL |
| 2 tbsp. | flour | 30 mL |
| 1/4 cup | amaretto liqueur | 50 mL |
| 2 | eggs | 2 |
| 1 1/4 lb. | purple plums, pitted and thinly sliced (4–5 large plums) | 625 g |
| 2 tbsp. | butter, cut into bits | 30 mL |
| 2 tbsp. | sugar | 30 mL |
| 2 tbsp. | toasted slivered almonds | 30 mL |

In a food processor, combine flour, icing sugar, and salt. Process briefly to mix. Add butter and process until mixture forms pea-sized pieces. With processor running, add egg yolk and gradually add ice water. Process until dough just begins to come together and will hold shape when pressed. Press into thick disk and roll out into a 12" (30-cm) round. Place over a 10" (25-cm) tart pan with removable bottom. Ease pastry over bottom and sides of the pan, pressing gently into place. Roll rolling pin over top of pan to trim excess pastry. Place tart pan on baking sheet and set aside.

In food processor, mix almonds, sugar, butter, flour, and amaretto. Pulse until crumbly mixture forms. Add eggs and process for 10 seconds. Spread mixture in even layer in pastry-lined pan.

Preheat oven to 400°F (200°C). Arrange plum slices in overlapping circles on filling (be generous). Be sure to fit plum slices tightly together. Cover filling completely. Dot plums with butter and dust with sugar. Bake 40 to 45 minutes, until tart has browned. Transfer to rack and let cool. Garnish with almonds. Serve at room temperature, with vanilla ice cream for the finishing touch.

Serves 8–10.

During the winter season there's little to be done outside, besides feeding and maintenance chores, so it's time for festive food indoors with the neighbours — a brunch or special New Year's dinner.

## Winter: Holiday season with friends

### Mid-day brunch with the neighbours

It's time to serve foods that comfort body and soul on the last day of the year.

### Super blueberry lemon muffins

| 2 cups | flour | 500 mL |
|---|---|---|
| 1/2 cup | sugar | 125 mL |
| 3 tsp. | baking powder | 15 mL |
| 1/2 tsp. | salt | 2 mL |
| | rind of 1 lemon | |
| 1 | egg | 1 |
| 1 cup | milk | 250 mL |
| 1/2 cup | butter, melted | 125 mL |
| 1 cup | fresh, frozen, or canned blueberries | 250 mL |

Topping:

| 1/2 cup | melted butter | 125 mL |
|---|---|---|
| 1 tbsp. | lemon juice | 15 mL |
| 1/2 cup | sugar | 125 mL |

Preheat oven to 425°F (220°C). Mix flour, sugar, baking powder, salt, and lemon rind in large bowl. Beat egg in medium bowl, then add milk and butter. Add egg mixture to dry ingredients. Stir until just mixed (batter will be lumpy). Stir in blueberries. Fill muffin pans 2/3 full and bake 20 minutes.

Topping:
Combine melted butter and lemon juice. Measure sugar in separate dish. Take slightly cooled muffins and dunk top into butter and then sugar.

### Apple cinnamon muffins

| 2 cups | flour | 500 mL |
|---|---|---|
| 1/2 cup | sugar | 125 mL |
| 3 tsp. | baking powder | 15 mL |
| 1/2 tsp. | cinnamon | 2 mL |
| 1/2 tsp. | salt | 2 mL |
| 1/2 cup | butter | 125 mL |
| 1 | large apple, peeled and diced | 1 |
| 1/4 cup | walnuts, finely chopped | 50 mL |
| 1 | egg | 1 |
| 2/3 cup | milk | 150 mL |
| 1 tsp. | cinnamon | 5 mL |
| 1 tbsp. | brown sugar | 15 mL |

Preheat oven to 425°F (220°C). Sift flour, sugar, baking powder, 1/2 tsp. (2 mL) cinnamon, and salt into large bowl. Cut in butter with pastry blender. Measure out 1/4 cup (50 mL) and reserve for topping. Add apple and nuts to flour mixture. Beat egg in a small bowl and add milk. Pour into flour mixture and stir until just mixed (batter will be lumpy). Spoon into lightly greased muffin pans — 2/3 full. Add 1 tsp. (5 mL) cinnamon and brown

in the bottom of a 10″ (25-cm) tube or Bundt pan. Decorate the bottom with pecan and cherry halves. Cream 1/4 cup (50 mL) butter and 1 cup (250 mL) brown sugar. Add eggs and vanilla. Beat until fluffy. Blend in sour cream. Mix flour, baking powder, baking soda and sift. Make a well in centre of dry ingredients, add liquids, and stir gently. Pour in greased pan and bake 30 minutes.

## Ham, fontina, and spinach strata (pictured on the left)

| | | |
|---|---|---|
| 1 | large baguette | 1 |
| 1/4 cup | butter, melted | 50 mL |
| 2 tbsp. | olive oil | 30 mL |
| 2 | medium onions, chopped | 2 |
| 1 lb. | piece of ham, cut into 1/2″ (1.5-cm) cubes | 500 g |
| 4 | large eggs | |
| 4 cups | milk | 1 L |
| 1 tsp. | salt | 5 mL |
| 1/4 tsp. | grated nutmeg | 1 mL |
| | pepper to taste | |
| 6 cups | fresh spinach, coarsely chopped (about 2 medium bunches) | 1.5 L |
| 3/4 lb. | Fontina or Gruyère cheese, grated | 375 g |

Preheat broiler. Cut baguette diagonally into slices 3/4″ (2 cm) thick. Brush both sides with butter and toast on baking sheet 3″ (7.5 cm) from heat until golden, about 30 seconds each side. Heat oil in large frying pan over medium-high heat. Add onions and stir until golden. Add ham and sauté until lightly browned. Set aside. In large bowl, whisk together eggs, milk, salt, nutmeg, and pepper. Add toasted bread and toss gently. Transfer saturated bread to shallow 3-quart (3-L) casserole, slightly overlapping slices. Place spinach and ham mixture between slices. Pour remaining egg mixture over all. Sprinkle Fontina over strata, lifting slices with spatula to allow cheese to fall between all slices. Preheat oven to 350°F (180°C). Bake strata in middle of oven for 45 minutes to 1 hour, or until puffed and edges of bread are golden and custard is set. This can be assembled a day ahead. Cover and refrigerate. Serves 6–8.

sugar to reserved topping mixture. Sprinkle over each muffin. Bake 15 to 20 minutes. Makes 16 large or 32 small muffins.

## Christmas coffee cake

| | | |
|---|---|---|
| 18–20 | pecan halves | 18–20 |
| 12–14 | cherry halves | 12–14 |
| 1/3 cup | butter | 75 mL |
| 1/3 cup | brown sugar | 75 mL |
| 1 1/2 cups | flour | 375 mL |
| 1 1/2 tsp. | baking powder | 7 mL |
| 1 tsp. | baking soda | 5 mL |
| 1/4 cup | butter | 50 mL |
| 1 cup | brown sugar | 250 mL |
| 2 | eggs | 2 |
| 1 tsp. | vanilla | 5 mL |
| 1 cup | sour cream | 250 mL |

Preheat oven to 350°F (180°C). Melt 1/3 cup (75 mL) butter. Add 1/3 cup (75 mL) brown sugar and stir. Place

## New Year's dinner with friends

Savour this meal as you reflect on the past year and think ahead to the year to come.

## Beef extraordinaire with sauce Diane

| 4 lb. | beef tenderloin | 2 kg |
| 1/2 cup | butter, melted | 125 mL |
| 3/4 lb. | mushrooms, sliced | 340 g |
| 1 1/2 cups | green onions, sliced | 375 mL |
| 2 tsp. | dry mustard | 10 mL |
| 1 tbsp. | lemon juice | 15 mL |
| 1 tbsp. | Worcestershire sauce | 15 mL |
| 1 tsp. | salt | 5 mL |

Leave tenderloin in whole piece. Preheat oven to 500°F (260°C). Place in pan on rack in oven for 30 minutes. Use meat thermometer — 30 minutes will cook beef to medium stage. While meat is cooking, sauté the mushrooms and green onions in the melted butter with mustard for 5 minutes. Add remaining ingredients and cook an additional 5 minutes. Keep warm on back of stove. Cut meat into thick slices. Serve with sauce. Serves 8.

## Perfect parsnips

| 3 | parsnips, peeled and sliced in matchsticks | 3 |
| 1 | carrot (for color), peeled and sliced in matchsticks | 1 |
| 3 tbsp. | butter | 45 mL |
| 1 tbsp. | lemon juice | 15 mL |
| 2 tsp. | fresh dill, chopped or | 10 mL |
| 1 tsp. | dried dill | 5 mL |

Stir-fry parsnips and carrots in butter over medium-high heat 3 to 4 minutes, until tender-crisp. Remove to casserole dish and sprinkle with lemon juice and dill. Serves 4–6.

## Potatoes rosti

| | potatoes, scrubbed, unpeeled (as needed) | |
| 2 tbsp. | butter | 30 mL |
| 2 tbsp. | salad oil | 30 mL |
| | seasoning salt to taste | |

Prepare potatoes using a melon baller (allow 8 to 10 balls per person) — leftover potatoes may be chopped and frozen for later use as hash browns. Parboil balls for 5 minutes. Drain. Preheat oven to 350°F (180°C). Put butter and oil in roasting pan and heat for 10 minutes; add potatoes and bake 45 minutes, stirring often. Drain on paper towel. Sprinkle with salt. These may also be cooked in an electric frying pan.

## Baked asparagus

| 1–1 1/2 lb. | fresh asparagus | 450–700 g |
| 3 tbsp. | butter or margarine | 45 mL |
| | salt and pepper to taste | |
| 2 tbsp. | lemon juice | 30 mL |

Preheat oven to 300°F (150°C). Rinse and trim asparagus — do not peel. Place asparagus in a shallow dish in one or two layers. Dot with butter and sprinkle with salt and pepper and lemon juice. Cover tightly with foil and bake 30 minutes.

## Onions stuffed with broccoli

| 3 | medium Spanish onions, peeled | 3 |
| 1 lb. | fresh broccoli | 500 g |
| 1/2 cup | grated Parmesan cheese | 125 mL |
| 1/3 cup | mayonnaise | 75 mL |
| 2 tsp. | lemon juice | 10 mL |

Preheat oven to 375°F (190°C). Cut the onions in half crosswise. Gently parboil in salted water for 10 to 12 minutes. Drain. Remove centres, leaving 3/4" (2-cm) walls. Chop centre portions to equal 1 cup (250 mL). Cook broccoli tops until tender-crisp; chop. Combine with chopped onion, cheese, mayonnaise, and lemon

## Aces

Chocolate nut crust:

| | | |
|---|---|---|
| 1 1/2 cups | crushed chocolate wafers | 375 mL |
| 1/4 cup | butter | 50 mL |
| 3/4 cup | crushed pecans or almonds | 175 mL |

Chocolate mousse:

| | | |
|---|---|---|
| 3/4 cup | chocolate chips | 175 mL |
| 8 oz. | cream cheese | 250 g |
| 1/4 cup | sugar | 50 mL |
| 1 tsp. | vanilla | 5 mL |
| 2 | eggs, separated | 2 |
| 1/4 cup | sugar | 50 mL |
| 1 cup | whipping cream | 250 mL |
| | chocolate curls | |

To make crust:
Preheat oven to 325°F (160°C). Combine chocolate crumbs and butter and press into a 9" (23-cm) spring-form pan. Sprinkle nuts over crust. Bake 10 minutes.

To make mousse:
Melt chocolate chips and set aside to cool. Blend cream cheese, 1/4 cup (50 mL) sugar, and vanilla. Beat egg yolks, add, and stir. Mix in cooled chocolate. Beat egg whites until soft peaks form. Add 1/4 cup (50 mL) sugar slowly and beat until stiff. Fold into chocolate mixture. Whip cream and fold into the chocolate mousse. Pour into springform pan. Cover and freeze overnight. Remove from freezer and refrigerate 5 hours before serving. Remove from pan and garnish with chocolate curls. Serves 8–10.

juice. Mound broccoli mixture in the onion halves. Bake uncovered in a buttered, shallow casserole for 20 minutes. Serves 6.

## Dill and Parmesan tomatoes

| | | |
|---|---|---|
| 3 | medium tomatoes | 3 |
| 2 tbsp. | butter | 30 mL |
| 1/2 cup | breadcrumbs | 125 mL |
| 3 tsp. | fresh chopped dill | 15 mL |
| | or | |
| 1 1/2 tsp. | dried dill | 7 mL |
| | salt and pepper to taste | |
| | grated Parmesan cheese | |

Cut each tomato into 4 slices and place on a cookie sheet. Melt butter, add breadcrumbs, dill, salt, and pepper. Spoon mixture onto each tomato slice. Sprinkle with lots of Parmesan. Place in cold oven under broiler (not too close) and turn on broiler. Keep an eye on it — cheese turns golden and crusty in about 5 minutes.

# A Salute to the Volunteers

Abbott, Andrew
Abbott, Fraser
Abbott, Fred F.
Abercrombie, Hart A
Abercrombie, Linda A
Aberle, Floyd
Abrams, Brian
Abrams, Edie A
Abrams, Joel
Acteson, Henry W.
Adams, Carolyn
Adams, Don
Adams, Rosanne
Adams, Ryan W
Adams-Wood, Alice
Adamson, Marian
Addley, Cy
Ady, Cindy
Agar, Gordon L
Ahloy, James
Airth, Bob
Aker, Audrey C
Aker, Eric E
Aldred, Glen
Aldred, Ross
Alexander, Greg
Alexander, Jean
Alexander, June
Alexander, Percy
Alexander, Wes
Algate, Betty J
Allan, Steve
Allen, Fred
Allen, Ray
Allen, Roy
Allery, Dave
Allison, Cathy
Allison, Glenn
Allison, Ted
Ambrose, R. Mark
Amery, Hiesem
Amthor, Carla
Amthor, Joan
Anderson, Bill
Anderson, Blake
Anderson, Dave
Anderson, Diane
Anderson, Donna K
Anderson, Fran
Anderson, Frances
Anderson, Frank J
Anderson, Guy R
Anderson, Heather
Anderson, Heather M
Anderson, John L
Anderson, Julie
Anderson, Marilyn
Anderson, Maurey K.
Anderson, Ron K
Andrew, Christine
Angus, Ian J.T.
Anselmo, Tony
Ansloos, Norma
Antoniuk, Brad
Antoniuk, Jodi
Antoniuk, Marlene L
Appleton, Stanley F
Archer, Fred
Archibald, Alan D
Archibald, Catharine
Armstrong, Art
Armstrong, Cathy

Armstrong, Chris
Armstrong, Doug
Armstrong, Fletcher
Armstrong, Jack
Armstrong, Melinda A
Armstrong, Tanya L
Arnold, Bob S
Arnold, John
Arthurs, Derek
Arthurs, Ric
Arthurs, Robin G
Ashbacher, Kelly
Ashbacher, Wendy S
Atchison, Sr., Bill
Atkins, Gordon A
Austen, Keath
Austin, Cynthia
Austin, Kimberly
Avey, Noreen P
Ayer, Andrea M
Aylesworth, Ken W
Aylesworth, Robert
Ayoungman, Angeline
Ayre, Gary
Ayre, Nate
Bacon, Keith
Bacon, Stephen R
Bacon, Terry
Badzgon, Jessica E
Bagby, Robyn
Bailey, Diane M
Bailey, Eleanor J
Bailey, Jim R
Bailey, Scott C
Bailey, Terry
Baillie, Brooke
Baillod, Brad
Bain, John
Baker, Diana E
Baker, Fred
Baker, Owen
Balazs, Patrick
Baldick, Karon
Baldick, Stephen
Ball, Bev A
Ballantine, Jane
Bamford, Bruce
Bamford, Kate
Bamford, Mary
Banadyga, Jarrod S
Bane, Nathan D
Baranieski, Hugh
Baranieski, Linda
Barby, Jim M
Barfuss, Milo
Barge, Ron
Bargetzi, Ernst
Barker, Donald
Barker, Geoff
Barker, Jay D
Barker, Pam
Barlass, Lesley
Barlow, Happy
Barrett, Gord A
Barrett, Marion A
Barrington, Gordon
Barritt, Angela N
Bartelen, Clarence
Bartlett, Erin S
Basarsky, Don
Bass, Marilyn L
Bates, Rick

Batke, Alfred
Batycky, Bill
Baxter, Allan
Baxter, Paula L
Beaton, Louise
Beattie, Al
Beaver, Lori
Beck-Edwards, Brenda
Bedford, Judy
Beeman, Denny
Beermann, Kari V
Befus, Dale
Belan, Chris
Bell, Andrew M
Bell, Cynthia
Bell, Herman J
Belot, Dan
Benedictson, Richard B
Benjamin, Karin
Benner, Beryl
Bennett, Barry I
Bennett, Kerrie
Bennett, Kristie L
Benning, Bernie
Benning, Maureen
Benoit, Chantale
Bentham, John
Bentley, Wally H
Beres, Garry B.
Bergeson, Judy A
Berglund, Donald James
Bertels, Frank
Bertram, Darlene
Bessem, Brian
Best, Kay
Beverley, Gareth
Bewley, John
Bews, Jim
Bews, Joy
Bezak, Erin
Bierwagon, Bruce
Big Plume, Louise
Biggelaar, Mike
Biggelaar, Ray
Bill, Tara
Billington, Rick
Bishop, Leanne M
Bissell, Judy E
Bittner, Sharon
Bjerstedt, Karen
Black, Cliff
Black, Michael
Blackburn, Jim
Blackburn, Les
Blakley, Lorne
Blood, Kathy
Blott, David
Blue, Bev
Boake, Bill J
Boake, Bud M
Boake, Peter
Bobenic, Jodi
Bock, Andre
Boisjoli, Sherry
Boisjolie, Dave
Bond, Nicholas
Bondarchuk, Alex
Bonke, Les L
Boomer, Barbara
Borland, Bob
Borrow, Patricia J
Boskers, Harm K

Boswell, Bob
Boswell, Jayne H
Boswell, Pat L
Bourne, Christopher
Boutestein, Jarrett
Bower, Sam M
Bowlen, Maureen
Bowman, Murray
Boyce, Carol
Boyce, Don G
Boyce, Gwen
Boyer, Colleen
Boyle, Randy
Brachman, Kirk
Bradley, Stu
Bradley, Tom
Brager, Joe
Brakke, Nancy L
Brasso, Donna K.
Brasso, Einar
Braun, Ed
Braun, Ilona B
Braunwarth, Garry
Braunwarth, Leta
Brayton, Joyce
Breaker, Nick
Breakey, Alan R
Brenda, Doug
Brennan, Jim S
Brewster, Amy A
Brewster, Jim
Brewster, Jolene
Brewster, Robert
Brimacombe, Peter R
Broad, Judy
Broadhurst, Michael
Brock, Bruce
Bromley, Bill
Bronconnier, David
Brookes, Mike
Brookman, George
Brookwell, Gerry
Browarny, Walt
Brown, Bill
Brown, Diana
Brown, Garth O
Brown, Gordon
Brown, Jack
Brown, John H.
Brown, Trudy F
Browne, Al
Browne, Irene A.
Bruce, David
Bryant, Linda L
Bryant, Victor
Buchanan, Deborah I
Buchanan, Gary N
Buchanan, Guy
Buckley, Margaret
Bucsis, Anita
Builder, Brenda L
Bunka, Andrew
Burak, Doris B
Burak, Heather J
Burgess, Ralph
Burgess, Sandra L
Burgess, Wayne B.
Burke, Brian
Burke-Gaffney, Kevin F
Burke-Gaffney, M. Eliza-
    beth
Burkowski, Janet A

Burns, Greg
Burns, James (Larry)
Burns, John
Burns, Rob
Burns, Shelly A
Burrell, Gord
Burrell, Mary
Burrell, Scott J
Burritt, Joe
Burwash, Les D
Burwash, Mary E.
Burwash, Sue A
Bushell, Beverley
Busse, Linda L
Bussey, Gordon
Bussey, Jim W
Busst, Bill H
Busst, Jack H
Butler, Dale
Bzeta, George
Bzeta, Judy
Cadre, Rhonda
Caines, Richard T
Cairns, Bob M.
Cairns, Gordon
Cairns, Ken
Calf Robe, Ed
Calf Robe/Ayoungman,
    Natasha
Callan, Lyne
Cameron, Bob
Cammaert, Pat
Campbell, Bill
Campbell, Doris
Campbell, John
Campbell, John C
Campbell, Kurt
Campbell, Laura L
Campbell, Linda
Campbell, Shannan
Campion, Lori M
Cannon, Dennis
Cantalope, Annette
Cardiff, John
Carels, Val
Carey, Frank G
Carey, Hugh
Carey, Neil
Carey, Trista
Carignan, Shannon D
Carpenter, Marcel
Carruthers, Bonnie
Carter, Kay C
Cartwright, Fred
Carver, Debbie L
Carver, Stan
Casey, Michael
Cashman, Larry
Cassels, John
Cassidy, Lynne
Cassie, Deanne J
Catellier, Shannon
Catherwood, Andy G
Cavanaugh, Buzz B
Celmainis, Sheryll
Chadwick-Lynch, Connie
Chalack, David
Chan, Leslie RH
Chapman, Ron
Charlton, Murton
Chartrand, Allan R
Chartrand, J. Aime

Cheetham, Rick E
Cherry, Gordon
Chisholm, Bill
Chisholm, Wynne
Chitrenky, Evelyn
Chitrenky, Walter
Chopin, Natalie
Chorney, Alan
Chorney, George A
Christensen, Dennis
Christensen, Lynn
Christie, Nat
Chu, Allan
Church, Andrea M
Church, Bob
Church, Lanny M
Clapham, Bill
Clapham, Kyle
Clark, Brendan C.
Clark, Cam
Clark, Jim
Clark, Lloyd J
Clarke, Bonny
Clarke, Jr., Eric G
Clarke, Sr., Eric
Clarkson, Linda
Claughton, Donald
Claughton, Mindy
Clay, Cam L
Clayton, Cody
Cleeve, Gail
Cleghorn, Dana
Coates, Joe
Coates, Warren S
Colborne, Barb
Coleman, Brian
Coleman, Karalee
Collins, Alison P
Collins, Bill E
Collins, Dave
Collins, Karen A
Collins, Michael
Collins, Pat
Colpitts, Garth
Comeau, Guy
Comeau, Val
Connelly, Dan B
Connelly, Sharleen A
Connolly, Luanne
Connors, Earl
Constable, Bob M
Constable, Loraine
Cook, Lorna J
Cooke, Darrell
Cooke, Don
Cooke, Grant
Cooke, Shane
Cooke, Sharon
Cooper, Jocelyn
Copeland, John
Copithorne, Danny
Copithorne, Jim
Copithorne, John G.
Copithorne, Marshall
Copithorne, Melba F
Corbett, Stewart
Cornish, George
Corraini, Debbie L
Corraini, Vallentina
Costello, Barry
Courtland, Christopher
Courtman, Ray

# A Salute to the Volunteers

Coutney, Bunny
Coutu, Marcel
Cowling, Lloyd G
Craig, Heather
Cranston, John
Cranston, Mary
Crawford, Q.C., George
Cremers, Devon
Cremers, Hans
Cremers, Maureen B
Cridland, Kelly
Cripps, Bruce
Cripps, Ron
Crook, Phil G.
Crook, Rhea
Crosbie, Wayne W
Cross, Donald
Cross, Eddie
Cross, Jill
Cross-Moulton, Sara J
Crowe, Leslie
Crowshoe, Reggie
Crowshoe, Rose
Crowther, Thelma
Cumming, Yvonne J
Cunningham, Bill
Cunningham, Debbie M
Cunningham, Lori
Cunningham, Norma
Cunnington, Mike
Cupit, Jackie L
Curran, Arlene
Curran, Mike
Curran, Jr., Stephen J
Curran, Sr., Stephen
Currie, Susan
Cushing, Don G
Cushing, Pat
Dahl, Cheryl A
Dahlgren, Nelson E
Daines, Grant
Dalgetty, David
Dalgleish, Dianne J
Dalgleish, Steve
Dalgleish, William
Dalgliesh, Judy L
Dalik, Dalton E
Dalik, Dorothy
Dalton, Rick K
Damm, Mark G
Danchuk, Jim
Dansie, Lynn
Danyleyko, Erin
Davidson, Brenda
Davidson, Debbie A
Davidson, Doug W
Davidson, Lori
Davies, Anne E
Davies, Arliegh E
Davies, Bob W
Davies, Don C
Davies, Ivan
Davies, Lynne A
Davies, Rowland
Davis, Arthur
Davis, Bill
Davis, Jay
Davis, Karen
Davis, Roger
Davison, John
Davison, Mike
Davison, Peter

Dawson, Darlene
de Haan, Brian
de Haan, Nick
De Looze, Hennie
Dean, Angela
Dean, Genevie
Dean, Jim
Dear, Don W
Debnam, Bruce
Debnam, Jess
DeCaria, Angela M
Decoux-Cozzi, Mark C
Deeg, Roger
Deeks, Kevin
Degenstein, Peter
Degenstein, Shirley L
DeMaere, Shauna M
Demmers, Ed
Dempsey, Hugh
Dempsey, Pauline
Dempson, Don
Denison, Robert
Dennis, Pat
Dennis, Sue J
Denoon, Barb R
Denoon, Norm S
Denoon, Stan W.S.D.
Derksen, Henry
Derksen, Kelly
Deschamps, Wayne
Desmarais, Georgia
Desmarais, Rene F
Desmarais, Tom
DesRochers, Johnnie
Dickie, Bryon K
Dickinson, Dave
Dickson, Myrna I
Didyk, Wayne
Dinning, Alexandra J
Dinning, Bob
Dinning, Jim F
Dinning Hughes, Heidi
Dixon, Dena M
Dixon, Howie
Dixon, Marilyn M
Dixon, Nicole
Dixon, Toni
Dodd, Arthur
Doherty, Brian
Doiron, Deedee
Doiron, Jan
Doiron, Lou A
Dokken, Carolyn
Dokken, Jim
Dola, Dale
Dolan, Regan
Dominick, Debbie L
Dominick, George
Domshy, Dennis
Donaher, Len
Donahue, Nimrodel
Donnelly, Rick
Dorais, Ginette
Doran, Jean
Dorran, Steve J
Dorsey, Everett
Dorsey, Mary Lynn
Doten, Vern
Dougall, Carol J
Douglas, Anne
Douglas, Ian
Doupe, Scott S

Douthwaite, Brian M
Downey, Cynthia
Downey, Deb
Downs, Kristi M
Dowson, Wayne R
Doyle, Joan D
Doyle, Joanne
Doyle, Kevin
Dragani, Joe
Drage, Heather L
Drake, Karyn
Drake, Kevin
Drake, Troy
Draper, Beth
Drever, Harry A
Drever, Jim
Drinnan, Sandy
Driver, Jean I.M.
du Berger, Brock
Duby, Clarende
Duchesne, Dale P
Duff, Neil
Duffin, Carrolle P
Duffin, Charlie
Duffin, Frank
Duffy, Gail
Duke, Ed S.M
Duke, Sonja
Dunbar, Brent
Duncan, Allen
Duncan, Les
Duncan, Randee
Duncan, Richard
Dunford, Anne E
Dunn, Holly A
Dunn, Jack
Dunn, Maureen
Dunn, Norma
Dunne, Hugh
Dunnigan, Sean
Dunsmuir, Scotty
Dupas, Giles A
Durant, Art
Durrant, Sandy
Dutton, Joe
Dvorkin, Harris L
Dwyer, Georgianne H.
Dyck, Bob
Dyer, Steven
Dygert, Edi
Dygert, Mike L
Dyler, Joe
Dyson, Dave
Dyson, Lynn
Eades, Ken G
Earl, Amanda
Earl, Carl
Earle, Thomas
Eastcott, Florence
Eastman, Lisa
Eastman, Tamie A
Eby, Orville R
Edge, Brian
Edge, Don J
Edge, Edith
Edge, Judy
Edwards, Eddy V
Edwards, Lorna
Edwards, M'Liss
Edwards, Steve
Edworthy, Gene
Edworthy, Marion

Egbert, Bill
Eggerer, Edwin
Eklund, Tanya
Elder, Mac
Elford, Clyde
Ell, Darlene L
Ell, Derrick
Ellingson, Don
Elliott, Sean C
Elliott, Susan
Ellis, Helen
Elman, Harold
Emms, Karen
Enderton, Lianne
English, Charles
Engstrom, Carol J
Engstrom, Edward
Engstrom, Jackie A
Enns, Ernest
Eremenko, Ron
Erickson, Milt
Erickson-Gess, Kathy I
Erion, Mark
Ernst, Breanna M
Erskine, Barry
Erven, Rita
Esson, Lindsay J
Estabrooks, Gary
Evans, Barbara A
Evans, Don
Evans, Judy
Evans, Kim
Evans, Kimberly E
Fahr, Dawn M
Fairbairn, Shanan R
Fairman, Rick T
Falck, John W
Fardell, Joe
Farley, Bunny D
Farries, Bob
Farries, Don
Fasoli, Debbie A
Fasoli, Robert L
Fath, Christie
Fawcett, Pam
Federucci, Alex
Federucci, Mira
Fee, Betti
Fee, Doug
Feist, Tracey
Felesky, Brian
Fennessey, Bill
Fennessey, Kevin
Fenton, Marjorie
Fequet, Joanne
Ferguson, Dwight
Ferguson, Glenna
Ferraton, Wanda
Fesko, Paul
Ficner, Henryk
Filippetto, Dean
Finley, Gail L
Finn, Frank
Finn, Graeme S
Finn, John
Finn, Nancy P.A
Finnman, Eileen
Finstad, Dean
Fior, Addiano
Fior, Michelle
Firmston, Larry
Fisher, Patrick

Fitzgerald, Sean
Fitzsimmons, Al
Fitzsimmons, Julie
Fitzsimmons, Terry J
Flaman, Terry
Flanagan, Debbie K
Fleischer, Clementine
Fleischer, Mike
Fleming, Jim K
Fleming, Kim W
Flewelling, Craig
Flundra, Dennis E
Flynn, Al L
Foged, Dave
Foo, Richard
Fooks, Robert T
Foote, Chris
Foote, Marv
Forbes, Ian
Forfylow, Idella
Forseth, Liz
Forster, Alex
Forsyth, Doug B
Forsyth, Gordon
Forsyth, Gregory
Fosado, Ramon
Foss, Art M.
Foss, Joseph
Fougere, Greg
Fougere, Tina
Fowler, Alvin
Fowler, Carol A
Fowler, Chuck N
Fowler, Harold M
Fowlie, Doreen F
Fox, Gwen
Fox, Wayne
Fraess, Bill
Franco, Karen
Fraser, Craig
Fraser, Diane
Fraser, Doug
Fraser, Kevin W
Fraser, Margaret J
Fraser, Peter
Frederick, Al D
Fremont, Charlotte
Frerichs, Earl
Friendly, David A
Friesen, Abraham
Friesen, Cory
Friesen, Leonard
Frotten, Clay
Fryers, Cliff
Fullerton, Dan
Fulton, Anita
Fyke, Lori
Fyten, Ron
Gabbs, Carelynne
Galatiuk, Elizabeth J
Gale, Bruce
Gale, Charlene F
Gale, Kendra
Gale, Ron
Gallais, Art
Gallaway, Joan
Gallelli, Gail P
Galvin, Donna
Galvin, Grady
Gamble, Rob G
Gant, Bill
Garberg, Brett

Garden, James
Gardner, Tracy
Garnett, Ralph E
Garwood, Douglas
Gathercole, Audrey
Gathercole, Brad J
Gathercole, Jim W
Gault, Kevin
Gearey, Dennis
Gearey, Margaret
Gee, Wing S
George, Hazel
Gerelus, Ken
Gernat, Kate M.
Gess, Bill
Gibbs, Gordon
Gibson, A.J.
Gibson, Ralph
Gifford, Peter
Giles, Dawn
Giles, Merv
Gillard, Mary I
Gilliland, Rex
Gillis, Shona J
Gillott, Bill
Gillott, Muriel
Gillott, Pat
Gilroy, Stewart
Gimbel, Murray
Gimbel, Veronica
Gingrich, Joel D
Ginther, Murray
Girling, Trevor
Gislason, Tammy
Giugovaz, Carole A
Gladstone, Terry
Glassford, Art R
Glenn, Leslie
Glimsdale, Donald
Glimsdale, Leigh-Anna
Glover, Cathy
Goldstrom, Dodie J
Gooch, Cory
Gordon, Barry
Gordon, Neil
Gordon, Roger
Gosling, David
Gothjelpsen, Tara L
Gottselig, Gerard
Gough, John
Gough, Vance P.J
Gould, Barry
Gowdy, Gordon
Grabatin, H.Dianne
Gracie, Brenda S
Graham, Bob
Graham, Bruce
Graham, Marg E
Graham, Marlene
Graham, Nan
Grainger, Donna
Grant, Don
Grant, Judy G
Grant, Kelly A
Gray, Bill M
Gray, Jennifer
Gray, Jim
Gray, Marcheta
Green, Bruce
Green, Ed
Green, Heather
Green, Jack W

ROPERS AT CALGARY STAMPEDE 1924
ALL USING FAMOUS PLYMOUTH ROPE
PHOTO

# A Salute to the Volunteers

Green, John
Green, Sandy
Green, Susan E
Greenslade, Joanne M
Greensword, Douglas
Greenwood, George A.
Grey, Lenn
Grier, Richard G
Griffin, Sharon
Griffith, Art
Griffiths, Terry R
Grimes, Kelly
Grisdale, Ted
Groeneveld, Charles
Groeneveld, Gaylene A
Groeneveld, Kim
Gromoff, Brian
Grove, Debra
Grove, Ken
Gruetzner, Sara-Jane
Gryckiewicz, Jan
Guay, Carol A
Gudmundson, Marge D
Guebert, David D
Guevara, Leslie
Guillemaud, Pat F
Guitton, Rick
Gulmick, Dawn J
Gunn-Allard, Joan
Guy, Vaughn
Hack, Kristin
Haeni, Adrian
Hagan, Edward
Hagerman, Allen
Hajash, Lorelei C
Hall, Doug G
Hall, Gary
Hall, Katherine A
Hall, Shannon C
Hall, Tom
Halliday, Martin
Halpen, Mary M
Halpen, Patty A
Halpen, Terry
Halpenny, Jay
Halseth, Gail
Halseth, Ross L.
Hamaliuk, Alan J
Hames, David
Hamilton, Bob B
Hamilton, Darol
Hamilton, Diane
Hamilton, Gavin
Hamilton, Leslie N
Hamilton, Sharon L
Hamm, Courtney
Hammer, Hoss
Hammer, Lorne G
Haney, Harry D
Haney, Shannon
Haney, Ted
Hanley, Irene
Hanley, Stuart
Hansell, Bob
Hansen, Joanne
Hansen, Kara L
Hansen, Reid
Hansen, Shawn
Hansen, Tim M
Hansma, Gerry A
Hanson, Wayne R
Harbour, Donna J

Harcott, Bill
Harcus, Wilhelmina
Harding, Larry
Harding, Peter
Harms, Paul
Harper, Don
Harper-Pollitt, Debbie
Harrington, Lorna P
Harris, Stewart
Harrison, Barry
Harrow, Darren
Harrow, Tracy
Harrow, Verna E
Hartall, Bill
Hartall, Wanda R
Harvie, John
Hasselfield, John
Hasselfield, Vel
Hatton, Sandra
Hauer, Craig
Hauser, Ernie A
Havelock, Ron P
Havens, Clint
Hawkwood, Aurica
Hawkwood, Eran
Hayden, Bill
Hayden, Vickie
Hayden, Yvonne T
Hays, Dan P
Hayward, Sylvia
Hazard, John
Hazen, Elsie L
Head, Jeannette P.
Head, Jennifer M
Headley, Neville
Healy, Earl
Healy, Harold
Heerema, Phil V
Heine, Charles
Heintz, Doris
Heintz, Maria
Helm, Rosanna
Helwerda, Denise F
Henderson, Doug
Henderson, Linda
Henderson, Patti
Henderson, Scott
Hendrickson, Keven
Henke, David
Henriksen, Raina
Hepburn, Bruce M
Hepton, Zoe
Herard, Rosalie A
Hermann, Dorothy
Hernandez, Art
Heskes, Justin F. R.
Hess, Archie
Hess, Marmie
Hess, Yvonne
Hewitt, Thomas
Hickey, Phil
Hiebert, Kathy
Hierons, Alison M
Hildebrandt, Jack
Hilderman, Jill E
Hill, Mike
Hill, Shirley
Hill, Terry
Hill, Wayne
Hills, June
Hind, John
Hinds, Ken E

Hironaka, Art
Hironaka, Brent
Hirsche, Grant A
Hitchner, Robert
Hlady, Mark
Hobbs, Bill H
Hobbs, Harry B.
Hobbs, Harry C
Hobbs, Harry N.
Hockley, Dallas C
Hockley, Trudy
Hodge, Brad
Hoeght, Judy
Hofbauer-Orr, Brenda
Hoffman, Dennis
Hofmeister, Marianna L.
Hogg, Kevin
Holbrook, Garry
Holbrook, Season
Holden, Robin
Holden, Shane
Holgate, Jayne M
Holland, Tannis L
Holloway, Eddie
Holloway-Savoia, Pam G
Holm, Art O
Holman, Len
Holman, Sally
Holmes, Bob
Holmes, Paul
Holmgren, Wayne
Holowatiuk, Bill
Holowaychuk, Robert
Holub, David M
Hood, Noriene
Hooks, John
Hoover, Bruce
Hopfner, Chris
Hornby, Ron
Horne-Price, Sandy L
Horton, Donna
Hoskin, Bert
Houle, Bob
Houle, Lynn
Hourie, Bill
How, Barry B
Howard, Ken
Howarth, Doreen
Howell, Ed
Howes, Steve
Hoy, Nelson
Hribar, Serena M
Hubbard, Bruce
Hubbell, John
Huddlestone, Dawn M.
Huffman, Kelly
Huggard, Susanne T
Hughes, Fred
Hughes, Jimmy
Hughes, Laura F
Hughes, Paul J
Huisman, Pam A
Hume, Brad
Hume, Ron
Humphreys, Greg
Hunt, Ray
Hunt, Ron
Hunt, Scott
Hunter, Karin
Huntley, Jim E
Hurlburt, K. Brant
Hurlburt, Ken

Hussey, Byron R
Hussin, Ken
Hutchin, Paul M
Hutchinson, Darlene E
Hutchinson, Reagan M
Hutchinson, Reid
Hutchison, Bev K.
Hutton, Hilary
Hutton, Jim
Hutzal, Jerry
Huyghe, Ken
Hyde, Janet
Hylton, Chris G
Hymas, Bob F
Hymas, Deen
Hymas, Rod
Iles, Marshall
Illingworth, Marie
Ingram, Robin
Innes, June-Marie
Iredale, Geoff A
Irvine, Will
Irwin, Art
Irwin, Carol
Irwin, Ian
Irwin, Ron
Isaac, Kay
Isaacs, Bev
Isakeit, Michael
Iversen, John
Iversen, Rita M
Jackson, Bill
Jackson, Dorothy
Jackson, Jeff
Jackson, Karen
Jackson, Pat
Jackson, Robert
Jackson, Ron A
Jackson, Sherry
Jackson, Todd
Jackson, Wayne
Jacob - Toews, Laurie M
Jacobson, Annabelle
Jacobson, Doran
Jacques, Don
Jacques, Nell
James, Cathie
James, Christie
James, Connie L
James, Dave E
James, Kaye
James, Patti Anne
James, Ron
James, Wes W
Jamieson, Doug A
Jamieson, Jeff
Janko, William
Jansen, Ted
Janz, Steven
Jaques, Diane
Jarvis, Roger
Javier, Jeff L
Jenkins, Bob
Jenkins, Jim H
Jenkins, Lee
Jennings, Roy
Jensen, Bob
Jessiman, Janet M
Jewitt, Ann M.J
Jewitt, Mike R.
Jinnah, Al-Noor
Joffe, Jay

Johnsen, Lisa
Johnson, Donna
Johnson, Greg
Johnson, Gus W
Johnson, Gustin
Johnson, Judy L
Johnson, Keith
Johnson, Mary E
Johnson, Sarah E.
Johnston, Brian
Johnston, Brian R
Johnston, David
Johnston, Isobelle
Johnston, Murray B
Johnston, Patricia
Johnston, Terry A
Johnston, Tracy
Jonassen, Amund
Jones, Brian W
Jones, Clarence
Jones, Karen
Jones, Keith
Jones, Keith B
Jones, Lorraine
Jones, Marvin
Jones, Ray
Joorisity, Shirley
Joosen, Peter
Jopp, Robert
Jorawsky, James S
Jorgensen, Tanya
Jorginson, George
Joyce, Raymond
Jubb, Avery
Judd, Glen
Judd, Reg
Juhasz, John
Juul-Hansen, Ivan C
Kaiser, Marilyn G
Kaiser, Wilf
Kalynchuk, Cathy D.L
Karch, Gordy
Karr, Avril L
Kaufmann, Bill L
Kavanaugh, Cory
Kavanaugh, Ken
Kazakoff, Dianne M
Kearns, Sheila
Keen, Douglas
Kell, Dan
Kelly, Marion
Kelly, Marise
Kemlo, Alison
Kemp, Gerry
Kemppainen, Leah
Kennedy, Dorothy
Kennedy, John H
Kennedy, Peter
Kenworthy, Shauna L
Kerby, George E
Kerr, Arlene
Kerr, Bob
Kerr, Sheila
Keshavjee, Sam M
Kewley, Bill
Kewley, Maureen
Khoury, Andrea M.L
Kidd, Alan
Kilby, Dave J.
Kilroe, Ken J
Kimmel, Brian D
Kinas, Jenny D

Kindrasky, Bev
King, David
King, Karin
King, Ken M
King, Madeleine
Kirk, Stacy
Kirker, Michael W
Kisilevich, Denise
Kitchen, Donna
Kitchen, Gerry
Kitz, Joan L
Kitzul, Grant
Klare, Frank
Klasky, Bill
Klasky, Bud
Klys, Jim
Knapp, Shelley A
Knapp, Victoria
Knight, Brenda
Knight, Bruce
Knight, John W
Knight, Susan E
Knorr, Maggie E
Knull, Betty J
Knutson, Debbie
Kollewyn, Hans JB
Kollewyn, Joan
Kolstad, Kate
Komitsch, Debbie
Konschuk, Shawn D
Konschuk, Wendy
Koop, David
Koper, Lawrence
Kortgaard, Joyce E
Kovitz, Jeff
Kozak, J. Fredrick
Kozun, Shawna
Krahn, Peter W
Krahn, Susanne
Kralka, Dan
Kranenburg, Lane
Krause, Jason K
Krauss, Shauna
Krawec, Randy
Kraychy, Cameron
Krebs, Darwin
Kristinson, Ray
Krivak, Derek
Kruyssen, Glenn K
Kryczka, Karen
Kryczka-McNear, Bev
Kunkel, Ed L
Kurtzweg, Vanessa D
Kwong, Sandy T.S.
Kyle, Doug H
Kyle, Kathryn I
LaBarre, Allan
LaBrash, Paul
LaBrie, Holly
Lacey, Lori
Lachman, Barbara A
Ladan, Terence
Laidlaw, Bob
Laidlaw, Joyce S.
Laidlaw, Rob
Laing, Laura L
Lam, Thien Minh M
Lamacchia, John F.
Lamont, Lisa
Lamoureux, Paul
Lamport, Brad
Lane Goodfellow, Cathy

# A Salute to the Volunteers

Lang, Dan M
Lang, Pam
Langford, Harry
Langford, Joan M
Langlois, Gaston L.
Lantz, David
Larsen, John A.
Larson, David E
Larson, Jim
Larson, Pat
Larson, Patricia
Larson, Terry N
Larway, Helene
Latour, Dorothy
Latus, Richard F
Lauder, David W
Lauder, Dianne
Laustsen, Ken D
Laustsen, Loraine
Lavalley, Gary
Law, Graham M
Lawless, Maureen A
Lawrence, Bruce A
Lawrence, Keith A
Lawson, Wayne H
Laycock, Bonnie L E
Leard, Scott H.M.
Leary, Howard
LeBlanc, Sandra
LeBoeuf, Gary G
Lee, Danielle
Lee, Darren R
Lee, Debbie E
Lee, Donald
Lee, Edmond Y.H
Lee, Gary M
Lee, Gary R
Lee, John A
Lee, Laura L
Lee, Ron
Lefevre, Chad D.
Lefley, Eileen P
Lefsrud, Lynette J
Legault, Tony H
LeGeyt, Chris
Lehr, Les
Leigh, Ron
Leighton, Barry N
Leitch, Robert E
Leitch, Robert O.
Lemay, Tara R
Lemire, Julie
Lengsfeld, Hans
Lennox, Al
Lennox, Ross
Lepp, Gordon
Lepp, Ren
Leroux, Carole C
Leslie, Jack
Leslie, Jason P
Leslie, Jean
Levangie, Nick M
Levitt, Fred
Lewis, Brenda
Lewis, Earl
Leys, Alan
Libin, Al
Liegman, Ed
Lietz, Lorraine M
Lindstein, Angie
Link, Allyson
Linklater, Suzanne

Liskowich, Trevor
Litke, Corene
Litke, Elaine
Littke, Zen
Little, Dianne E
Little, Norman
Lively, Allan
Livingstone, Wendy M
Lloyd, Bill J
Loades, George W
Locke, Charlie
Locke, Louise
Lockwood, Stephen
Loewen, Katherine
Loken, Solveig E.
Loney, Carol M
Longeway, Dave
Longeway, Eric
Longeway, Ray
Longman, Gerry
Longman, Patricia
Longmoor, Val A
Longmore, Jake
Loor, Clinton
Lorenz, Diane
Louden, Judy
Lougheed, Dave
Lougheed, Peter
Love, Maurice
Lovig, Rob
Lovse, Marg
Low, Mike
Luchsinger, Brian T
Luft, Richard
Lukey, Orest
Lund, Joe
Lundberg, Stacie M
Lunn, Alana
Lutz, Jackie
Lutz, Jim
Lutz, Katie
Luxford, Paul
Lyle, Candace
Lyle, Mark LK
Lyle, Rick
Lynch, Jim
Lynn, Ken
Lyon, Wayne
Lyon, Wendy L
Lyzenga, Jennie P
MacCallum, Andy
MacDonald, Brian
MacDonald, Bruce
MacDonald, Dan C
MacDonald, Gerrie
Macdonald, Howard A
MacDonald, Laurie
MacDonald, Rich S
Macdonald, Stu
MacEachern, Nancy
MacFarlane, Craig D
MacFarlane, Cynthia C
MacInnes, Richard
MacInnis, Don
MacIntyre, Amanda L
MacKay, Heather
MacKay, Murray
MacKellar, Lucille
MacKenzie, Dean
Mackenzie, Judy E
MacKenzie, Michelle
MacKenzie, Susan C

Mackie, Doug
Mackin, Bill
MacKinnon, Grant
Mackintosh, Lachlan
MacPherson, Don
MacRae, Jenn S.
MacRae, R. Gary
Madsen, Marian E
Madson, Arron
Maertens-Poole, Carole Anne
Magee, Neill
Magnon, Arlene L
Magnuson, Tom
Mailman, John P
Main, Evelyn
Major, Steve
Maki, Linda
Malenica, Peter M
Malette, J.P. Scotty Pierre G.G.
Malin, Gerry M
Malin, Susan
Mallabone, Guy
Mallabone, Joan
Maller, Dave A
Maloney, Jack
Mamchur, Gary
Manarey, Bill H.
Mandeville, Bryan
Many Guns, Doris
Markert, Ron T
Markkanen, Brian
Markowsky, Sandy E
Marshall, Bill H
Marshall, Ed S
Marston, Jan
Marston, Maureen H
Martin, Dick
Martin, Fraser
Martin, Greg A
Martin, Moyra
Martin, Todd
Martindale, Shannan
Martinson, Ryan J
Martyn, Ian
Martyn, Kari J
Martz, Warren
Marx, Doris
Mate, Jorge
Matejka, Steve
Matheson, Tom
Matthews, Chris R
Matthews, Geoff R
Matthews, Kay
Matthews, Rob
Matthews, Tim
Matthews, Tom
Matticks, Geoff
Matuska, Ron
Mawer, Martha M
Maxie, Peter
May, Dan A
May, Joel A
May, Ron A
Maynard, Tina
Mayson, Bill
McAllister, Patrick
McArthur, Doreen
McBride, Jim
McBride, Rod
McCabe, Tom

McCafferty, Brenda
McCallum, Joan
McCarthy, Larry
McCaughan, Glen L
McCauley, Ted
McClellan, Dale
McClellan, Grace
McClellan, Reg
McClelland, Craig
McClelland, Keith S
McCollister, Gus
McConnell, Kim
McCorquodale, Larry J
McCosh, Ron K
McCuaig, Bob
McCune, Pat
McDaniel, Rod
McDonald, Alan K
McDonald, Bruce A
McDonald, Carol M
McDonald, Don W
McDonald, Erin
McDonald, Gertrude
McDonald, Glenn B
McDonough, Steve
McDonough, Terry E
McDougall, Michael
McEwan, Maureen
McGowan, Gil
McGrath, Peter
McGregor, Don
McGregor, Kevin
McGregor, Kim
McInnis, Ken W
McIntyre, William Robert
McIver, Ric W
McIvor, Jack
McIvor, Mike
McKay, Carol
McKay, Elaine K
McKay, Jack
McKay, John
McKay, Melissa
McKay, Scott
McKendry, Roxanne L
McKenna, Darilyn
McKey, Michael S
McKinnon, Allison
McKinnon, Colin A
McKinnon, Don J
McKinnon, Jane
McKinnon, Teri K
McKinnon, Wayne C
McLachlan, Brian A
McLane, Herb
McLaren, Barbara
McLaren, Wayne
McLauchlan, Ronald
McLaws, Donald
McLean, Elfie L
McLean, Janet E
McLean, Joan
McLean, Ward
McLellan, Neil
McLellan, Sheila
McLeod, Lynn
McLeod, Rod
McMahon, Terry
McMillan, Ian
McMillan, Les
McNamara, Carol E
McNeil, Kirk

McNeilly, Steve
McPeak, Jim
McPherson, Carol S
McVean, Bruce
McVicar, Jeanine
Meadows, Patricia L
Meck, Iris
Meers, Scott
Melbourne, John
Melchior, Ron J
Melnechuk, Alex
Melville, Judi M
Mercer, Lisa
Merrick, Bernice
Merrick, Bob
Merrill, Derek
Meyers, Janice
Mezzarobba, Marilyn E
Michaels, David
Mick, Lorne
Middleton, John
Midtdal, Tamy
Milavsky, Harold
Millar, Roberta
Miller, Bev
Miller, Don
Miller, Doug
Miller, Jamie
Miller, Lindsay
Miller, Pam
Millican, Harold S
Milligan, Jim L
Mills, Bonny
Mills, Brett
Mills, Judy
Mills, Paul J
Milne, David
Milne, Jo-Anne C
Milne, Marlie D
Milton, Helen
Miner, Dorothy
Ming, Dennis R
Minnes, Patsi
Mirdoch, Julie A
Mish, Bernie M
Mitchell, Esther C
Mitchell, George
Mitchell, John
Mitchell, Randy
Mjolsness, Mary E
Moffatt, Greg
Moffitt, Barry
Mogridge, Bill
Moir, Dianne
Molesky, Joanne
Molnar, Marnie
Montana, Pete
Monteith, Bill
Moody, Bob
Moon, Graham
Moore, Bob
Moore, Don
Moore, Fred J
Moore, Greg W
Moore, Jim K
Moore, Jody
Moore, Ken
Moore, Kirk
Moore, Wayne
Morasch, Clinton
Morasch, Loyde
Morgan, David R

Morgan, Faron
Morgan, Robert C
Morison, Sheila
Morissette, Ron L
Moroz Clarke, Janet N
Morozoff, Lloyd W
Morrill, Bill
Morrill, Cherlyn
Morris, Julene C
Morris, Norm
Morrison, Alexander C.
Morrison, Graydon
Morrison, Keith
Morrison, Kim
Morrison, Murray B
Morrison, Neil H
Morrow, Ed N
Morsky, Marsha
Morton, Ray
Mouser, Ross
Mrozek, Ed
Mryglod, Glenn D
Mueller, Gladys
Muir, Leigh
Mullett, Roy
Mulyk, Brenda M
Mundie, Drew
Munro, Al
Munro, Barry G
Munro, Jim
Munro, Roy A.
Munro, Shannon
Munstermann, Chris
Munstermann, Mel A
Muri, Welland
Murphy, Joanne G
Murphy, Karen
Murphy, Kelly L
Murphy, Paul
Murray, Brian
Murray, Chris E
Murray, Russell W
Musich, Rudy
Musselwhite, John A
Myers, Cheryl M
Myketyn, J. Eric
Myketyn, Kathy
Naegeli, George
Nahachewsky, Tammy
Napke, Stephanie
Neis, John
Neis, Joyce E
Neis, Todd
Nelles, Frank R
Nelson, Diane
Nelson, Doug
Nelson, Kevin
Nelson, Ralph
Nelson, Val
Nesbitt, Jack
Nesbitt, Tricia
Nesselbeck, Barbara J
Neuman, Pat
Newby, Wayne
Newman, Gillian
Newman, Paul
Newman, Peggy
Newman, Peter E
Niblock, Leanne
Nicholls, Jon S
Nicholls, Patrick
Nicholls, Pepper

# A Salute to the Volunteers

Nickel, Clarence
Nickel, Kathaleen E
Niederwieser, Harold
Nield, Bill
Nielsen, David A
Nimmo, Bryce
Noble, Vern E
Noonan, Alexandra
Norcross, Don
Norford, Brian
Nummela, Linda A
O'Connor, Graham
O'Connor, Larry
O'Connor, Michael J
O'Connor, Mike J
O'Connor, Sandy M
O'Connor, Stuart G
O'Connor, Tom
O'Leary, Thomas
O'Meara, Erin
Oades, Arthur
Oatway, Don J
Oberg, Margaret
Oblak, Kathy L
Odnokon, Mick
Oelke, Ken D
Olasker, Sonny
Oman, Tracy L
Ona, Wally E
Ondrik, John
Onerheim, Joan
Opsal, Cindy
Orchard, Peggy
Ornburn, Marilyn R
Orr, Lea
Orr, Richard B
Osborne, Barbara
Oseen, Shauna
Osler, Jock C
Osler, Will
Ostashower, Shirley
Oulton, Brandy P
Owad, Don A
Owad, Judy
Owen, Jeff
Owens, Tom
Paget-Turcotte, Twyla
Pahl, Lorena
Pallesen, Peter
Palmer, Cec
Palmer, Ella
Palmer, Jim
Palmer, Rose M
Panes, Ann
Panes, Gabriel
Pappas, K.C.
Pardo, Cindy E
Park, Bob
Parker, Karen
Parker, Shirley
Parkhill, Don J
Parry, Liz W
Parsons, Don
Paterson, Leigh
Paton, Bert
Patterson, Amanda P
Patterson, Frederick
Patterson, Tony
Pazdor, Philip
Peacock, Fred
Peacock, Jack R.
Peacock, Jim

Peake, Colleen
Pearce, Gordon
Pearson, A.J.
Pearson, Pat A
Pearson, Robert V
Peatz, Jason S
Peckham, Travis
Pedden, Allan
Pedersen, Annemarie L
Peers, Dana A
Peers, Rick
Pelletier, Marylyn
Pendrel, Annice
Pendrel, John
Peneycad, Fiona M
Penner-Collins, Denise H
Penny, J.C.
Peplinski, Jim
Percival, Trina B
Percy, Leanne D
Perizzolo, Rudy
Perry, Dale G
Perry, Lynn L
Pestun, Janice
Peters, Jack
Peters, Leigh A
Peters, Nancy K
Peters, Rob
Peterson, Rod C
Petrie, Leslie J
Petryk, Pat
Phillips, Dave
Phillips, Ross F.
Phillipson, Roxanne
Phoenix,
Pidde, Paul
Piercy, Lauren E
Piers, Bill
Piers, Susanne
Pigott, Maryann
Pilling, Gary M
Pilling, Jim
Pilling, Merv L
Pinder, Roy
Piper, Jennifer M
Pitt, Judy
Pittman, Mac
Planche, Don R
Platt, Donna M
Platt, Gordon S
Platz, Anne V
Plunkett, Tom
Poffenroth, Bob
Poffenroth, Donna F
Pogue, Bob
Pokrandt, Dave F
Polischuk, Debbie
Pollock, Bonnie S
Polowick, Marlin
Polson, Paul
Pope, David
Popik, Leon B.
Popik, Leon C.
Poratto, Adele
Porter, Arlene
Porter, Bill
Porter, Patricia Y
Porter, Ray T
Postlewaite, Don
Postlewaite, Scott
Potter, Jacqueline L
Poulton, Patricia

Powder, Kevin
Powell, Nathan
Powell, Stan
Powers, Jim
Poyen, Jock
Preece, Derek
Presley, Christel M
Presley, John W
Prettie, Andy
Price, Al
Price, John
Price, Stacy L
Pringle, Bertram
Pringle, Sandra
Pritchard, Collin
Pritchard, F. Vicky
Pritchard, Herb
Pritchard, Rob
Proceviat, Ashley E.L
Prodan, Dean
Prodan, Hugh
Prokosch, Lynn M
Proskie, Joe
Proskow, Darrol J
Proskow, Morris
Prosser, Ernie
Proud, Jennifer
Puffer, Bruce
Purcell, Gordon L
Purdy, Carl
Purdy, Glen
Purdy, Kirk
Purdy, Storm
Pyke, David
Quarrie, Ron
Quinney, Bill
Quinton-Campbell,
    Patricia
Raby, Stephen G
Racher, Garth
Ralston, Brenda J
Ramsay, Graeme
Ramsay-Carlson, Kaye
Ramsden, Dick
Rasmussen, D. Heather
Rasmussen, Gordon
Rawlyck, Donna
Rayner, Ruth Ann
Rebalkin, Darren
Rebeyka, Frank S
Redmond, Bruce
Reeb, Fred
Regehr, Pamela J
Regehr, Rod
Reglin, Yvonne
Reid, Stuart J.A.
Rempal, Garrett
Reynolds, Anni L
Reynolds, Clive
Reynolds, Colleen A
Reynolds, David
Rhodes, Darryl
Richards, Adele
Richards, Mick
Richardson, Allan
Ricketts, Lisa N
Rieberger, Michael
Riley, Tim A.
Rimer, Barry
Rimer, Luke J.
Riopel, Cherie
Risdon, Marlene

Ritchie, Randy
Rivers, Joanne
Roach, Joanne
Roach, John
Roach, Matt
Robak, Brian
Robak, Liliana
Roberts, Donna
Robertson, Garry J
Robertson, Jim
Robertson, Keith
Robertson, Pat A
Robertson, Robert
Robertson, Ron
Robertson, Sharon E
Robertson, Shawna
Robinson, Carla
Robinson, Dave
Robinson, Gay
Robinson, Jean
Robinson, Tyler
Robinson, Val A.
Robinson, Wayne E
Robinson Ladiges, Cathy
Robson, Dave
Roche, Barbara
Rockafellow, Donna
Rodgers, Lonnie
Roe, Kerri L
Rogers, John Victor
Rogers, Mike R
Rogers, Ron
Rogoza, Sandra
Rojo, Angie
Ronald, Brent
Rook, Gordon
Rooney, Len
Root, Karen L
Root, Mayne
Roscoe, Dick
Rosia, Tanner
Roska, Van
Roska, Vince
Ross, Bob W
Ross, Carl H
Ross, Jack
Ross, John R
Ross, Katherine
Ross, Marilyn M
Ross, Mike
Ross, Shirley
Ross-Albert, Alison
Rothermal, Kevin E.
Rourke, Mac
Routley, Don
Rowe, Ralph
Roy, Bruce
Royal, Ted
Rudd, Dave
Ruddell, Terry N
Rude, Kevin
Rugsven, June
Rule, John
Rule, Lynn
Runcie, Garnet D
Russell, Dan
Russell, Ken
Rusted, Brian
Rutherford, Keith
Rutherford, Paul W
Rutley, Howard
Rutley, Kirk

Ryder, Larry
Sabo, Russ
Sadowski, Rob
Sahs, Dennis M
Sailor, Stan
Saju, Sherali
Saklofske, Harold
Salomons, Gordon J
Sampson, Tom
Samulak, Shaunna
Sanden, Al W
Sanderson, Greg L.
Sanger, Neil
Sargeant, Donna
Sattin, Allan
Saucier, Heather A
Saunders, Alf
Saunders, Bill
Saunders, Fred W
Saunders, Steven
Saunders, Wendy
Saunderson, Jana
Sautner, Linda
Savage, Garry
Sawchuk, Dianne
Sawchuk, Ron
Scheirman, Brian
Schild, Olive
Schmaltz, Doug
Schmelzl, Frank
Schmiedchen, Christine
Schmiedchen, Gay C
Schneider, Jack
Schneider, Jessica F
Schneider, Mark
Schneider, Jr., Jack
Schofield, Maggie A
Schreiner, Duane A
Schuelke, Lara
Schuh, Rick
Schultz, Barb
Schultz, Tom
Schultz, Wade
Schulz, Maureen B
Schunicht, Oliver C.
Schwarz, Bob
Schwieger, Ron
Scobie, Shannon D
Scott, Bob
Scott, Ivy
Scott, Peter
Scott-Brown, Diane
Screaton, Anne M
Seabrook, Keith
Seaman, Dennis E
Sears, Bev
Seifert, Jim
Seifert, Opal
Seitz, Blaine
Selgensen, Eric
Selgensen, June
Semotuk, Lydia
Sergerie, Cindy M
Seto, Fong
Seto, Richard H.
Sevick, Russell
Sewall, Brad T
Sewall, Kim E
Shacklady, Ted M
Shalanski, Karen
Shandro, Douglas
Shanley, John R

Shannon, Shilo
Shannon, Todd
Shaver, Grant
Shaver, Inez L
Shaw, Bev A
Shaw, Gardie
Shaw, Kirk
Sheane, Paul
Shearer, Jim
Sheka, Tenzin
Sholdice, Marnie
Short, Valdine J
Shurmer, Byron
Shute, Dennis
Shute, Ed
Shuttleworth, Wayne
Sibbald, David
Sibbald, Wayne M
Sicotte, Nicole M.J
Sietzema, Hidzer
Silliker, Frank D
Sim, Darrel K
Simmons, Shane
Simpson, Dave
Simpson, Dixie M
Simpson, Joseph R
Sinclair, Brian
Sinclair, Odell
Sinton, Terry R
Sitting Eagle, Gerald
Skaggs, Rick A
Skeans, Paul
Skeels, Dan
Skupa, Tom
Slade, Don J
Slater, Gordon
Sledzinski, Brenda
Slocombe, Robert
Sloman, Lance
Smith, Alison
Smith, Amy J.
Smith, Bunny L
Smith, Carole F
Smith, Craig
Smith, Debbie
Smith, Donna L
Smith, Ernest
Smith, Gregg
Smith, James P.
Smith, Jean
Smith, Jim
Smith, Laura
Smith, Paulette A
Smith, Quincy
Smith, Rick
Smith, Robert G
Smith, Sean
Smyth, Sean
Snow, Gary J
Snow, Stacie E.
Snyder, Steve
Soltys, Deanna
Solvason, Corie
Solvason, Lorne D
Solverson, Larry H
Somerset, Blake R
Sorensen, Grethe
Sorensen, Jette
Southern, Ron
Sowiak, Christine F
Sparling, Stan
Sparrow, Bert

Calgary Stampede
—1926—

# A Salute to the Volunteers

Spear, Herb H
Spence, Dwayne
Spence, Roc D
Spence, Shayne A
Spohr, Becky
Spooner, Sharon A
Sprague, Bob H
Spratt, Jane
Spratt, Nancy A
Sproule, Courtney
Sproule, Katie
Sproule, Mark R.
Squires, Paul D
Staddon, Sean
Stafford, Rod F.
Stainsby, Esther M
Stainsby, Kim
Stanlake, Allison
Stanton, Dan
Starchuk, Richard
Stark, Marguerite
Starlight, Bruce
Starling, Louise
Stearns, Don
Steblecki, Ben
Steedman, Cliff
Steel, Jim S
Steele, Barbara J
Steele, Heather
Steen, Jack
Steen, Patsy
Steen-Bowles, Laurie D
Stefanchuk, Peter
Stefanchuk, Thora B
Steiner, Brian
Stella, Dean
Stephen, Marian
Stephens, David
Stephens, MaryL
Stephenson, Barbara B
Stephenson, Dan
Stephenson, George
Stevens, Mark
Stevenson, John
Stewart, Carol D
Stewart, Don
Stewart, Don
Stewart, Doug
Stewart, Frank D
Stewart, Frank G.
Stewart, Hilary
Stewart, Holly
Stiles, Sharon
Stilwell, Vic
Stirling, Rob M
Stirling, Shannon
Stitt, Jim G
Stock, Carol
Stockwell, Robert
Stone, Ruth A
Stott, Kate
Stott, Ken G
Stout, Bill
Stout, Don
Stout, Shane
Strandlund, Christy
Strandquist, Halley
Strange, Michael
Straub, Shane
Street, David
Street, Glenn
Strem, Tracy

Strem, Vince
Stricharuk, Jack L
Stroick, Mike
Stroman, Fred
Stuart, Al
Styles, Barry
Suddaby, Darrel L
Suddaby-Johnson, Tara D
Sullivunn, Kaye
Sumner, Bill E
Sumner, Bob
Sumner, Joan
Sunderland, Vyetta
Suto, Angela
Sveen, Joan
Sveinson, Keith
Swanby, Erik
Swanson, Al
Swanson, David F
Swanson, Francine
Swanston, Don J
Swanston, Donna
Swanston, Linda J
Swinton, Bill
Switzer, Cathy M
Switzer, Clay E
Switzer, Sam
Symons, Bill
Symons, Marilyn
Syvenky, Steve
Tainsh, Dave L
Takenaka, Larry T
Takken, Connie
Talbot, David
Tanner, Dorothy
Tanner, Lynn
Tanner, Monti
Tarbox, Lori
Targett, Bryan
Taubert, Tracy
Taylor, Beth
Taylor, Bill
Taylor, Brian J.
Taylor, Ellie M
Taylor, Eric T
Taylor, Fred
Taylor, Freddy M
Taylor, Ken
Taylor, Lyle
Taylor, Morley
Taylor, Paul
Taylor, Robert
Taylor, Robert
Taylor, Stan B
Taylor-Flexhaug, Myrna L.
Tegart, Happy
Thachuk, Shelley
Thacker-Bjarnason, Sis
Tharp, Bernard
Thevenaz, Dave
Third, John
Thomas, Jane M
Thomas, Lance N
Thomas, Linda
Thompson, Bob
Thompson, Bonnie
Thompson, David
Thompson, Debbie
Thompson, Don L
Thompson, Jack
Thompson, John
Thompson, Lee

Thompson, Len
Thomson, Monty W
Thomson, Patricia G
Thon, Wendy
Thorbjornsen, Tracy
Thoreson, Julie
Thoreson, Roy
Thorne, Bill S
Thornton, Dolores V
Thornton, Harold P
Thornton, Lynne
Thorpe, John
Thrasher, Kate D
Tickles, Ed J
Tickles, Laurel E
Tidball, Bill D
Tidsbury, Isabella E
Tidswell, Kim M
Tidswell, Sandy J
Tilley, Wayne
Tillie, Della
Tillman, Sharon
Tilly, Michelle
Tittemore, Jim A
Tobert, Owen
Todd, Averil M
Todd, Bill
Toft, Gary
Tomilson, Susan M
Tomlin, Denean M
Tomlinson, E. Dale
Tomney, Sue J
Tomshak, Mike
Torgerson, Gary
Tornberg, Carol
Tough, Allan
Traquair, Brad I
Treacy, Bob
Treacy, Donna
Treacy, Linton E
Trimble, Harvey
Troughton, Josie
Tuck, Philip
Tucker, Mike
Tucker, Ron
Tull, Don G
Tupper, Dave V
Turel, Rocky R.
Turnbull, Glen B
Turner, Don
Turner, Henry J
Turner, Jeanette
Tveter, Orlo
Twittey, Herb S
Twittey, Margaret L
Tynan, Bill
Tynan, Colleen J
Tynan, Maureen
Tynan, Russ
Tynan, Wendy M
Tyrrell, John
Tyrrell, Michele
Vajdik, Marcel
Valentine, Megan
Valentine, Pat
Valentine, Peggy
Valentine, Peter
Valliere, Lynda
Van Dyck, Peter
Van Erkel, Ben
van Gilst, Sarah T.R.
Van Ham, Jim

Van Laar, Barry
Van Maarion, Christina
Van Mierlo, Dianna
Van Staden, Chris
Van Tighem, Peter
Van Tighem, Tammi
Vande Walle, Leo
Vanderwiel, Art J
Vanderwiel, Christopher
Vanwalraven, Marlena
Venini, David J
Vennard, Gene R
Verbonac, Debbie
Vesey, Bob
Vetere, Mario
Viccars, Bob
Vickery, Gary A
Villeneuve, Alain
Vincelli, Douglas
Vine, David
Vipond, Grant
Virostek, Blaine
Visser, Arlene
Vogel, Ron E
Vogelsang, Annette
Volk, Amanda
Volk, Connie
Waddell, Linda
Waddell, Wayne
Wagner, Erle
Waldorf, Don
Waldron, Keith
Walker, Bob
Walker, Cam
Walker, Drexel B
Walker, Edward
Walker, John
Walker, Patti L
Wall, Ron
Wallace, Bob
Wallace, Chris
Wallace, Darla R
Wallace, Don
Wallace, Donna
Wallis, Laurie
Walsh, Bill
Walsh, Tom
Walters, April
Walters, Bret
Warawa, Kathryn
Ward, Deborah D
Ward, Ron
Wardner, George B
Ware, Bob
Warga, John
Warren, Janice A
Waters, Mark D
Watmough, Rusty M
Watson, Colette S
Watson, David R
Watt, Gerald
Watt, Ian
Watts, Bill J
Watts, Dawn
Way, Bill
Wearmouth, Sue-Anne
Wearmouth, Vicki L
Weaver, Harold A
Weaver, Ross
Webb, Connie B
Webb, Kathleen
Webber, John W

Webster, Gordon
Weerstra, Marjorie M
Weidner, Arlene A
Weiler, Gary J
Weir, Meryl B
Weir, Rob
Weismose, Norm
Welch, Irene
Weldon, Owen M
Welsh, Larry J
Werbisky, Mike
Werle, Stephanie C
Wesner, Tara
West, Fred E
West, Gordie
West, Kim
Westerberg, Eric
Westerberg, Lyndon
Westerson, Joan S
Westlund, Jamie L
Wetherup, Hal
Wetherup, Jackie M
Wetherup, Michael
Wettstein, Carl H
Whenham, Donn
Whenham, Robin
Whenham, T.O.
White, Bob
White, Terry
White-Tucker, Kerry
Whitfield, Jason
Whitlie, Geoff
Whitworth, Jack
Whitworth, Marion
Wichmann, Annette
Wiebe, Horst G
Wiebe, Vic
Wiegman, Henry J.
Wiens, Heather
Wiersma, Annelies
Wiese, Brian S
Wiggan, Al
Wight, Hunter
Wildman, Brett
Wilkes, Perry T
Will, Marilyn D
Williams, Bruce
Williams, Gloria
Williams, Jack
Williams, Judy
Williams, Len
Williams, Lennie
Williams, Mark J
Williamson, Keith M
Willoughby, Teri
Wilmot, Fred
Wilson, Bill
Wilson, Bob
Wilson, David K
Wilson, Dick
Wilson, Don
Wilson, Don
Wilson, Ehren
Wilson, Helena
Wilson, Linda
Wilson, Penny
Wilson, Robert
Wilson, Shawn
Wilson, Steve
Wilton, Sheldon
Wimmenhove, Cindy-Lee
Wimmenhove, John

Windolff, Gladys M
Winkler, Evelyn C
Winters, Natalie
Wise, Keith D.
Witbeck, Bill
Wittmann, Diane
Wonderham, Peter J
Wong, Sam
Woo, Harvey
Wood, Barry
Wood, Gerry J
Wood, Laurel
Woodall, Stephen
Woodward, Marian
Woolrich, Earl
Woolstencroft, Dorothy M
Worobec, Barb
Wosnock, Ken J
Wray, Doug
Wright, Allen H
Wright, Allison
Wright, Cam A
Wright, Donald
Wright, Lexi A
Wright, Lorelei
Wright, Murray
Wroe, Barry
Wudrich, Deanie F
Wyatt, Donna
Wylie, Justian W.
Wylie, Kelly
Wylie, Len J
Wylie, Tiffany J
Wyse, Donna
Yakunin, Alex
Yeast, Bill
Yeast, Sharon
Yee, Marlaine
Yee, Wee
Young, Betty
Young, Beverley
Young, Don J
Young, Doug
Young, Graham
Young, Jereme
Young, John
Young, Karen
Young, Robert
Younker, Tania L.
Yuffe, Hartley
Yule, Janet
Zaytsolf, Gloria
Zboya, Donald G
Zell, Ray
Zeran, Peggy
Zickefoose, Sherri
Ziegler, Earl
Ziegler, Kathleen
Ziegler, Sandy
Zimak, Tracy T
Zipse, Dean
Zipursky, Brad
Zukerman, David
Zwick, Dan

# A Salute to the Full Time Staff

ABRAMENKO, EDITH
ABUGAN, DAVE
ADJEI, JOSEPH
AGER, STEVE
ALEXANDER-MCBRIDE, DEREK
AMES, SANDY
ANDERSON, GORDON
ANDERSON, GRACE
ANHORN, ALLISON
ANHORN, MICHELLE
ANNEAR, TOM
ARMITAGE, DOUGLAS
ARMSTRONG, GARY
AXELSON, KEN
BABIN, LAURA
BADGER, AARON
BAIN, GARRY
BALABAS, LARYSSA
BARKER, NEIL
BARLARO, PAULA
BARNES, JODI
BARTEL, MITZI
BARTLEY, JO-ANN
BASQUE, ELIZABETH
BASQUE, VERA
BASSETT, DOUG
BEAUCHAMP, RITA
BECK, DAVID
BELL, BEN
BELLINGHAM, JAMES
BEWS, TONY
BLACHFORD, CAMERON
BOESCH, CARRIE
BOWIE, PEGGY
BOWLEY, DOUG
BRETON, ROGER
BURGE, KIM
BURWASH, ROBIN
CAIRNS, ROBERT
CAMOZZI, WENDY
CAMPANELLI, BRETT J.
CAMPBELL, JAN
CAREW, RONALD
CARR, BRENT
CARRUTHERS, BONNIE
CARSON, SHAUNA
CARTER, MARILYN
CHAPMAN, JENNIFER
CHITTICK, BRIAN
CHMIEL, LAURA
CLARKE, LISA
CLEGHORN, DANA
CONNELL, WARREN
COOK, JOANNE
COUTURE, BRENDA
COX, BEVERLY
CRAWFORD, TERRILL
CROOK, LAWRENCE
CRUMB, CORTLAND
DALE, DEREK
DAVIS, CHERYL
DAVIS, DIANA
DAWLEY, DAWN
DEAKIN, DAVID
DEANS, RAND T.
DEBAIE, ROGER
DEBOER, CYNTHIA
DEBOER, WES
DELANEY, MICHAEL
DEMMERS, RAE ANN

DIAKOWICZ JIM
DIRK, GARRY
DOBER, HOLLY
DOLHAINE, HILARY
DONALD, GARY
EBBELS, TANNIS
ELIAS, ROY
ELLIOTT, DAVID
ENS, RICK
ENS, WENDY A.
FACHE, GORDON
FERGUSON, DEBRA
FINCH, CHERI
FOGLEMAN, WENDY
FORSETH, DWAYNE
FORSYTH, HAROLD
FOSTER, STEVEN
FOURNIE, JACKIE
FRASER, DOUG
FREIDAY, LLOYD
FRIESEN, MIKE
FRITZ, MAX
GAAB, COLLEEN
GABRIEL, PAUL
GALLINGER, KENNETH
GALLOWAY, LINDSEY
GALOC, CARMEN
GANLEY, JOAN
GARNETT, SHARON
GARNETT, GORDON
GENEST, DARCY
GEORGE, MATTHEW
GLEASON, TIMOTHY
GOEMANS, BART
GOLL, DEAN
GOODMAN, RAYMOND
GRAY, CHARLES
GRISAK, GEORGE
GUERRERO, MARIA
GUTOWSKI, MICHAEL
HAGEL, PAM
HANCHAR, BRENDA
HARRISON, PAUL
HARTFORD, DIANA
HASPER, DAVID
HASPER, CRISTINA
HAUSER, DEBORAH
HAWLEY, SUSAN
HAYNES, GRANT
HEADLEY, ANTHONY
HENNING, ROBERT
HESS, HOWARD
HICKMAN, DAVID
HIGDON, GERRY
HISLOP, NEWTON
HOBART, JAMES
HODGINS, JACK
HOEHN, ANDRIA
HOLDEN, LINDA
HOLM, JENNIFER
HOLMES, SHERI
HORPINUK, DUANE
HUNT, PATTI
ISKRA, EDWARD
IWANYLO, OREST
JAMES, JAYNIE
JARDINE, LINDSAY A.
JEAL, TED
JEANNOTTE, KIMBERLEY
JENSEN, CAROLINE

JOHNSON, BJORN
JOHNSON, STEVEN
JOHNSON, JODI
JOLLIMORE, PAULINE
KAMITOMO, AARON
KELLY-GRAVELLE, EILEEN
KENDRICK, TIM
KIMBALL, VERNON
KINDEN, COREY
KING, WILLIAM_J
KNIGHT, KEN
KOHINSKI, LOUIS
KUNIMOTO, KIMBERLY
KUSINSKI, JOANNA
KWONG, WILLIAM
LACHAPELLE, JACQUELINE
LACOSTE, MICHELLE
LADHA, ANAR
LALIBERTE, PAUL
LANDRA, MARGARET
LAURENDEAU JAMES
LAWRENCE, PETER
LAWSON, CANDACE
LAYCRAFT CATHERINE
LEAVITT BRIAN
LEE, KEITH
LITTLEY, SHIRLEY
LONGMUIR LINDA
MA PAUL
MACEACHERN TOM
MACHISKINIC, DOREEN
MACISAAC, OLIVERA
MACLENNAN, LISA
MAERZ, CHANTELLE
MAPE, REY
MARKLUND, CATHY
MARRINGTON, KEITH
MARTIN, BILL
MATTILA, LISA
MAYO, KIMBERLEY
MCAFEE, SANDY
MCCABE, SEAN
MCCANN, EMILY
MCCARTHY, GREG
MCCARTHY, MAUREEN
MCCLEARY, CATHERINE
MCCULLOUGH, KIRK
MCFADZEN, MARTY
MCGRATH, ANITA
MCGRATH, BARRY
MCHUGH, GERRY
MCINTYRE, LINDA
MCNEIL, NEIL
MCQUEEN, BRADLEY
MEDING, VERN
MENKS, ANN-LOUISE
MERCER ,TYLER
METZ, PATRICIA
MILLIONS, TARA
MILLS, SHARON
MORRISON, MONIQUE
MORROW, PAUL
MUENCH, MARK
MULLIGAN, KEVIN
MURFIN, TERRY
MUSGRAVE, ROBERT
NEARING, LAURA
NEWINGER, DONALD
NICHOLSON, JAYNE
NIEBERGALL, DARREN

O'NEIL, JOHN
OLIVER, GARRY
PALOSANU, GEORGE
PASCOE, GORDON T.
PATRAM, SHERRY
PAYNE, WALTER
PEARCE, ED
PEDERSEN, MIKE
PENNOYER, KELLEY
PON, PATRICK
POOLE, GAIL
POWLAN, GAY
PROUDFOOT, ROD
PYNE, ANN
RACETTE, GAIL B.
RADKE, JAMES
RAMAGE, ALAN
READ, TRACEY
REHILL, KEN
REID, MITCHELL
REID, TRACY
RICE, J.T.
RIZZUTO, JUDY
ROBBINS, JOANNA
ROBINSON, GRAEME
RODGERS, KENNETH
ROGERS, BONNIE
ROHL, STEPHEN
ROSENBERG, PAUL
ROSS, ERIK
RURAK, TERRY
SAARENOJA, JOUNI
SABOURIN, TODD
SAVIC, NADA
SCHEIDT, DARLENE
SCHILD, LAURIE
SEWELL, DAVID
SHARP, MIKE
SHAW, NEIL
SIMMONS, GAIL
SIMPSON, HAL
SITTER, VALERIE
SLOF, JEFF
SMITH, DARRYL
SMITH, STEPHANIE
SNOWDEN, BARRY
SOBULIAK, CATHY
SPECKEEN, LONNIE
SPEEDY, ANGELICA
SPREEMAN, GRACE
STANG, LESLEY
STEELE, DAVID R.
STEELE, SUSAN
STERLING, BRIAN
STEWART, DAVE
STEWART, DON
STICKLEY, ROBIN
STUTSKY, TRACY
SUEL, CHERYL
SUGDEN, JENNIFER L.
TAN, ISAAC
TEARE, DONALD B.
THEN, TRACY
THOMAS, GERALD
THOMAS, LORI
THOMPSON, KEVIN
TINKLER, KERRIE
TO, KIM
TOCHENIUK, BEV
TOCHENIUK, SHANNON

TROTTIER, ALYNN
TURSIC, SAFETA
VAN GELDER, RICHARD
VASTAG, SANDOR
VOTH, SHIRLEY
VUONG, ANNE
WARDER, BRETT
WATSON, LESLIE
WEBB, SUSAN
WEIDINGER, CARRIE
WEIR, CAROLE
WEISS, JORDANA
WHITNEY, AMANDA
WHITTINGHAM, MARC
WHITTLE, MICHAEL
WIEBE, TIMOTHY
WILLISTON, JAMES
WISE, ROBERT
WITTUP, JACKSON
WOJTAS, SLAWOMIR
WOOD, LAUREL
WOZNY, JEANETTE
WRIGHT, ALLISON
WRIGHT, BRUCE
WYATT, JEFFREY
YEADON, SUE
YEAST, SHARON
YOUNG, JIM
YOUNG, PEARL
YUONG, NORMAN
ZALAPSKI, ADINE
ZBYTNUIK, JERI-LYN

Please note: Volunteer and Staff names are from the 2005 roster.

# Index

Note: Page numbers in italics refer to photographs.

# Photographic Credits